Mind of the Mystic

I0110635

Mind of the Mystic

Glen A. Just

Published by Eagle Entertainment USA

130 Teton Lane #2

Mankato, Minnesota 56001

Website: www.eagleentertainmentusa.com

ISBN: 978-098-3205-708

Table of Contents

PROLOGUE

MINOR GODS:

ALTERED STATES OF CONSCIOUSNESS REVEALED

Mind of the Mystic is a sequel to *Autobiography of a Ghost*. In *Ghost* I explained how altered states of reality (ASR) and altered states of consciousness (ASC) are created, controlled and can be directed by us individually once we understand how these mystic experiences emerge from our minds. My autobiography of abuse and trauma documents how I discovered altered states that we commonly call speaking in tongues, shamanic spirit possession, flying out-of-body or astral travel, reincarnation, group visions and collective drug trips, automatic writing, and experiencing the presence of ghosts.

I explained how altered states emerge naturally from our own minds, and that altered states are intra-psychic phenomena and not of supernatural origin. The following chapters will elaborate on the emergence of altered states and how they can be called up at will, controlled and directed. Once again, I reference my personal history to provide a roadmap for those who wish to call forth altered states from their own minds, or who simply desire to understand these long misunderstood phenomena.

My personal history has taught me that people of different religions frequently resent having ASC brought out of the closet. Throughout most of human history altered states have been associated with divine communication. Generally, individuals who most strongly resent discovering that altered states are just another expressive form internal to the human brain are adherents to major world religions, or True Believers in shamanic practices; individuals who see these states as critical to their own beliefs in the supernatural.

It is logical for True Believers to ask: If my religion's prophets or shamans were just experiencing modified inter-neuronal connections when they were having visions or experiences central to their beliefs, ASC that were used to create an understanding of God or gods, then the basis for my religious beliefs may be called into question? If I can create, control and direct similar altered states and mystic realities, am I also a prophet or shaman? Can religions that are founded on uncommon but normal brain functions that reflect the culture of a specific time be a true reflection of God's design, or are they something of a lesser nature? Are we our own demigods?

The fact that we can create, control and direct an altered state does not answer the question of God in any final way. What knowledge of this creative process does, however, is to show us how our minds are the source of these naturally altered realities. In the same manner that we no longer believe that evil spirits make us sick, or that the Earth is the center of the universe, is it possible to continue believing that speaking-in-tongues or flying out-of-body is bringing us into contact with the supernatural when we are just experiencing unusual configurations of our own neural networks? Can we believe that historical mystics performing these feats were any more in contact with the Divine than we are when we duplicate these experiences?

The positive side of unmasking ASC for the True Believer is the realization that natural explanations bring us one step closer to understanding ourselves as human beings and helps us more fully come to know our own spirituality. Personally, I have found this process of unmasking ASC gratifying because it eliminates most of the tension created by the current debate between theism and atheism – God versus the Blind Watchmaker. You need not fear losing God by understanding mystic phenomena, and you will probably come as I do to sense a new integration, a new wholeness of being that will leave you increasingly open to Gardner's *The Intelligent Universe.* Once we emerge from the cave of not knowing, the larger universe becomes more, not less wonderful.

The gap between religion and science, which has become a huge divide for many, begins to close and we are left with the unanswered questions raised by works like *The Intelligent Universe.* If you believe in the Divine, you have moved a step closer to knowing your God, and if you are an atheist, you have moved a step closer to understanding your own nature. Each belief system of God or No-God is brought to the next level of understanding. And standing shoulder to shoulder, theists and atheists must ask: What evidence do we now have for either position? The answer becomes one of near equality.

I have argued in *Ghost* that religious experiences are built into our DNA and suggested that we are foolish to deny that they are a fundamental part of what higher life forms evolve into. I strongly suggested in *Ghost* and elaborate in *Mind of the Mystic* that denying the spiritual part of our humanity gets us into more trouble than acknowledging our innate religiosity. Further, ignoring our mystic capacity as atheists do, a capacity that is expressed when we create new neural pathways in our brains, reduces understanding of how we become more ethical beings and limits a fuller understanding of how the Universal Moral Code emerges to become part of a mature psyche.

I suggest that by continuing this ignorance we are more likely to destroy each other through hate than we are to build a larger world and universe of love. By mastering ASC, we come to know that we human beings create the visions of self-destruction that we use to kill and demean each other. We are responsible for these actions and can no longer blame war and genocidal acts on interpretation of gods or God that we build from our minds. I am not saying that we have simply built God from our minds, but rather, that we have built gods of limited ability from these intra-psychic experiences whether they are by shamans, monotheists or trinitarians.

I take the position that hard atheism of the Dawkins variety compounds our inability to create a harmonious world by denying this most fundamental part of our human nature. My position supports removing interpretations of historical mysticism that have been used to explain common but misunderstood mental functions, thereby freeing us to explore our religious nature in accordance with the natural laws of the universe. Or, as Francis S. Collins says in *The Language of God* when he writes of evolution as one of God's scientific facts:

"But that says nothing about the nature of the author. For those who believe in God, there are reasons now to be more in awe, not less (Collins, 107). Paraphrasing Collins, God's instruction book creates our mental and psychic functions as a result of this same evolutionary expression. I ask the reader to demystify altered states of reality and move one step closer to understanding his or her own human nature, and to be open to exploring what is really out there in this great universe of ours.

Atheism stops the search that leads us to a more complete understanding of ourselves and our spirituality. Rather than state as Dawkins does that religion is an illusion and the greatest source of conflict the world has ever known, the reverse becomes obvious – that denying our own religious nature, which includes the mechanisms that give us these experiences, stops us short of an adequate understanding of ourselves. It is not possible to breach our varied understandings of a multitude of interpretations of mystic experiences until we comprehend their origin and misuse. I am arguing that ignorance of how our own minds work is the source of this conflict.

Ignorance of how mystic experiences are created in our minds is to be feared as a major source driving the hatred that separates all humanity as sisters and brothers; a force that permits atheists to hate non-atheists, and theists to hate atheists. These experiences have been with us throughout human history, and will not go away just by accepting the position of the atheist that religion is wrong or illogical, or of accepting the position of the theists that their specific brand of dogmatism is the correct interpretation. My central argument is that our religious nature is to be engaged, understood, explained and used for the betterment of everyone on this planet.

In similar fashion, dogma by polytheists or monotheists, by individuals of major world religions that build support for their favorite prophets on naturally emerging altered states of reality, or mystic explanations for natural creations emerging from our brains, run the same risk as the atheists: Denying normal functions of our human psyches leaves the religious dogmatist in an equivalent position of denying natural causes for ill health. They are in a position of declaring that the world is still flat.

When we discovered natural causes for illness, our lives became better, not worse, and we rejoiced in saving lives, removing pain, and curing illness. The hand of God, or if you chose, the algorithms in our DNA, working through free will were increasingly embraced as we used our innate capacities to improve our lives and our world. We are blind when we first step out of the cave and cannot see clearly, but come to love the light.

In *Ghost,* I demonstrate my own struggle to become whole, my struggle to bring together a fragmented self, and the steps taken to achieve this integration. Extreme abuse and neglect produces damaged human beings with fragmented psyches and I was once one of these individuals. I initially came to reject religious explanations for the world when I encountered their endless conflicts and the illogical contradictions in and across world religions. As I struggled for wholeness, I initially grasped the most logical explanation available to me. The only explanation that removed contradiction and provided an improved logical philosophy was that all religions were wrong, leaving atheism as the only answer.

However, the problem that atheism created for me was its inability to explain my own mystic experiences. Tension was reduced by accepting this belief of non-belief and finding it no longer necessary to eliminate religious contradictions, although larger tensions and contradictions beyond those found in major religions were not eliminated. Thus, I continued to search. The limitation of atheism that I found most debilitating was its denial of my own experiences and spirituality. I had to deny much of who I was and how my brain operated, and I had to deny the fact that our knowledge of the universe is incomplete. I had to pretend to actually know the universal design of the cosmos, but I increasingly became uncomfortable in this state of denial.

In religion, in science, in philosophy and in life, we are driven to resolve our own cognitive and psychic conflicts, because it is human nature to create meaningful explanations for all that we experience. For many of us, ASC are part of our natural experiences and beg explanation. These mystic experiences cannot be simply dismissed by pretending that they do not exist, or are part of mental delusions, or are part of false beliefs. Evolution, what is in our DNA, does not permit premature closure of this emergent life force. In *Mind of the Mystic,* each of these issues is developed, and I add a few facts from science. I will draw more extensively from neural science and neural philosophy to continue clarification of the gaps left by *Ghost* as I continue to unravel mystic experiences.

Finally, there are a few basics from psychology and neural science that I considered in my own passage from mental illness to health. A quick review of abuse and neglect as our brain structure is altered will be considered in respect to spirit, mind, and body integration. Integration occurs naturally and almost automatically as we remove psychic dividers, and is necessary if we are to become mature adults. This integration is inevitable as we move up the ladder of consciousness to embrace the Universal Moral Code.

1 - REALITIES IN OUR PSYCHES

THE REALITY OF DEATH EXPERIENCES

The division between Heaven and Earth, altered reality experiences taking place in our own brains, often puzzle us, and we want to know what these images mean. The distinction between what is natural and what is supernatural has not always been easy to make. In *Autobiography of a Ghost*, I conclude with a series of insights in the Epilogue that place altered reality experiences in our psyches. I demonstrate how I discovered mystic experiences of intra-psychic origin and noted that this reality is sometimes threatening to True Believers who have always placed altered reality experiences common to their religions as coming from God or the supernatural. Death experiences have been commonly viewed historically as representing a moment when we touch the Divine. It may be a shock to realize that we can account for these experiences as something that is naturally taking place in our own minds.

What I experienced as a young child at two years of age when I consciously refused Heaven was totally real. There was no logical contradiction between what was external and what was in my mind. What was happening in the world outside of my mind and what was happening in my mind were equally real and interchangeable. I have shared in *Ghost* that realities

1

created in our minds are just as clear and convincing as those coming from the outside. Unless we take a closer look at how our mind operates, we continue to believe we have met the angels, God, the gods, or whatever supernatural world our culture tells us exists. I will analyze these experiences to see how we can differentiate between these two realities.

In the same sense of total reality when I met the angels, my Genesis Journey, where I go to the beginning of time and the beginning of the universe, was experienced as being equally real, even though I made the journey over sixty years later after I had a lifetime of experimenting with altered realities. However, in contrast to my toddler experience, I consciously set up the Genesis Journey, enjoyed it fully, and knew that I had created it and was controlling the experience. The entire trip was experienced as though I had actually left my body and traveled to the beginning of time and the beginning of the physical universe. In my Genesis Journey I traveled back almost fourteen billion years to the creation of space and time. It was an incredible trip, and it left me spellbound for a number of days.

I know now, and I knew then, that God was not directing my Genesis Journey. It was not a vision given by the Divine Being. It was just me having fun on a cold winter's day, and exercising a capacity that many of us have, but a capacity that is not common to all.

Historical figures have gone out on the ice, into the desert, to the mountain tops, or subjected themselves to great stress before their supernatural visions emerged. This was also the case for me when I was a toddler, and my first out-of-body experience was triggered by trauma. But what leads me to believe my toddler death experience was entirely natural?

Without the hindsight of sixty plus years of living and education, I believed my dying in the hospital at age two actually brought me into contact with angels. I left my body just as I had for the Genesis Journey, and floated between my father and the nurse both when leaving and returning to my body. I consciously refused Heaven, remember passing through the sheet to re-enter my dead body, and had a vivid image of the angels. I revisited this experience many times as I passed through my childhood years. It remains an image that is completely real; an image similar to that of my father attempting to chop of my brother's head with an axe. It is a very clear and distinct visual picture that lives permanently in my mind. If the Other Side speaks to children in a manner that can be understood by a two year old through everyday images familiar to the child, then it was a true vision of Heaven. On the other hand, what are the clues that the vision came entirely from within my own mind?

Images stored in my young mind were from my world of everyday experiences. The angels were dressed like the young adults who were taking care of me. They were similar to aunts and uncles in age and appearance and just floated through the air toward me. None of the angels were older or were children. There was no vision of Heaven opening up with streets of gold or other marvelous signs that are sometimes reported by others having similar death experiences. I noted in Ghost that my hospital bed was placed in a manner that permitted me to look past my hospital room door into the stairway, and that it was so placed that I didn't see people's feet as they walked toward me. They just seemed to float. The angels floated toward me in a similar fashion. My mind was accessing stored images from my two year old brain.

When my Uncle Gus died some months before my death in the hospital, I vaguely recall family talking about his death and going to heaven and what a great place heaven was, a world without pain. It was a place of eternal comfort protected by God and a future home we could all look forward to. What was perplexing then was the reality of my memory which reproduced the perspective of leaving my body, being at the same height as my father, nurse and doctor, plus having this visual, mental picture of my sheet-covered body. I was also conscious of passing through the sheet upon returning to my body. These are totally real experiences and the reader will have little difficulty understanding how convincing they are to a two year old boy. But all the imagery came from my world with the cultural interpretations of Heaven by adults in this world.

Glen A. Just

I made no conscious effort to leave my body. I first remember hearing that I was "gone," and the next instant I felt as though I was standing, not floating, between my father and the nurse. Then, the hospital scene vanished and twinkling, distant lights became my complete mental picture. Next, the twinkling lights acquired bodies as they came closer and individual features emerged for males and females who were all about the age of Dad, aunts and uncles. There were no words spoken that I recall, but the thoughts were clear, and I knew that they were angels coming to take me to Heaven. I felt warmth and love coming from them as they came with outstretched arms. I learned later that the twinkling lights that I experienced are common to many who have death experiences. It is associated with oxygen deprivation and brain damage as the brain struggles to continue working. It also occurs when the brain rearranges inter-neuronal connections during these episodes.

Just before the angels physically embraced me, I decided not to go with them to Heaven. I turned my back on them, and seemed to pass through a cloudy or opaque shroud as I returned to my position between Dad and the nurse. I observed my sheet-covered body once more and then decided to get back into it. At that moment, I did not think about how I was able to pass through the sheet. Later as I thought about reentering my body, the sheet seemed to pose a problem. How did I pass through it? As a child, I was never bothered by the problem of getting out of my body or returning to it because I always felt as though my body and spirit remained together. This is a typical experience of mind-body being one with out-of-body travel.

After returning home, similar out-of-body experiences often took place and felt just as real as they did in the hospital. Out-of-body projections that let me pass through solid objects were never a problem throughout my lifetime. And as I recounted in my autobiography, when the movie "Ghost" came out, I thoroughly enjoyed moving through physical objects with the actor (ghost) as his actions were animated in the film. When we are still at a naïve level of understanding, we struggle to make sense of these experiences. My child mind knew that people do

4

not pass through physical objects, only spirits can do this, but my child's mind still demanded an answer.

Later in life, by age eight, I found the out-of-body experience of passing through the roof of my house to be equally curious. How could I do that? I even practiced passing back and forth through the roof to see if I could feel it, but as a child I never understood how it worked. To my inner reality, my body accompanied me on these childhood journeys as it had during my toddler death. When I became an adult, I was aware that my flesh and bones remained in place as my psyche (soul) escaped its physical body and took flight. Even so, my psyche experienced being attached to my body, for intra-psychic altered experiences still use the body as reference. How else could it be? (Lakoff & Johnson, 1999) We do not store physical images in our mind that have no substance. Even ghosts, at minimum, have a filmy essence. Eventually I came to distinguish between flights of the spirit (soul) and what was actually happening to my physical body. This awareness did not fully come into being for me until my college days at the University of Minnesota: When I began to practice self-hypnosis, I became fully aware of controlling the process and consciously experienced the mind--body distinction under my control.

In Collective Trips, as I recount in *Ghost,* I give an example of a group of young men sitting on an iceberg that has been projected from their minds and experiencing the ice's coldness on a hot summer day. The experience taking place in their minds duplicated a real iceberg well enough that they experienced relief from a hot summer's day. That's reality! The young men had orchestrated the iceberg affair, hence, were aware of their own control and never claimed that they had entered another world that was made up of ice and the supernatural. They simply shared a collective drug trip. The uninformed psyche does not make these distinctions as the intra-psychic reality duplicates all the senses to create an experience of being there and actually feeling ice.

In Collective Shamanism I recount my own experience with the Native American Church where I visually witnessed the soul of a departed brother, the brother of a good friend, returning to and standing by the fire pit during his honoring ceremony. This experience was just as real as that described by my "collective trip" students. Group induced experiences are just as real as individual ones, and our psyches act in tandem with others. Those who are unable to imagine dozens or hundreds of people collectively enjoying the same trip believe the experience to be real because it involves so many others. They take the group experience as proof that supernatural forces are at work. Group hypnotists ply their skills on large numbers of people, and their ability to work with groups can be commonly observed. This is a practice that predates the Christian calendar in ancient Egypt. Consequently, historical accounts of group spirit visitations offer no more credible explanations for spirit visitations to us the living than individual experiences do. Magicians who practice illusions achieve these effects without drugs or hypnosis. The Romans of Jesus' Era labeled them magicians not prophets.

Group and individual hypnotism was imported from Egypt and came to the Middle East before the time of Jesus. Hundreds of self proclaimed prophets were nailed to the cross for being practitioners of magic around the time of his crucifixion. Obviously, this army of prophets was not sent by God to redeem our sins as they languish in obscurity. Nevertheless, they must have been a threat to the local authorities who persistently killed them for disturbing the public order. The influence brought by prophets from Egypt and other parts of the world must have been considerable to crucify so many. Clearly, the population of Jesus' time readily believed in and extensively participated in these magical practices.

Experiences within our psyches, psychic experiences, can as easily be collective as they can be individual. Nevertheless, when groups collectively report visions, the phenomenon is given additional credibility. Large numbers of observers with similar visions have been taken to mean Divine visitation. It must be real, because a hundred people reported the same experience. We cannot make this assumption by numbers alone as we come to understand collective trips and collective shamanic experiences.

Once we unveil the origin of our altered reality experiences through natural mechanisms we are not permitted to go back and use pre-scientific explanations. In similar fashion, we cannot argue that disease is still caused by bad spirits. We cannot argue that bloodletting improves health. We cannot argue that the Earth is the center of the universe. We can no longer argue that God created the world is six physical days of 24 hours and then rested. Instead, one argues that new knowledge changes our interpretations.

We move from darkness to enlightenment, but always there is another rung to the ladder. My point: we also move closer to an understanding of how both our psyches and nature operate, thereby coming to know what is really out there in this Intelligent Universe. We stop defining the natural order, and begin to accept it for what it is.

OUT-OF-BODY EXPERIENCES

In Halfway to the Moon from *Ghost,* I describe my eight year old trip to sit on the moon as a reaction against my father's attempt to chop my older brother's head off with an axe. My brothers' near death experience instilled fear that I might become a victim of Dad's raging temper. Let me analyze this astral trip from an adult perspective, an analysis that I believe must be applied to other similar mystic out-of-body experiences in literature that assume supernatural explanations. I recall my emotional state well when Dad was trying to get Brother Bud's head on the chopping block and cut it off. I was physically immobilized from fear, but recall that I wanted to snatch the axe from his hand and prevent my brother's death. But Dad had conditioned me to expect being hit by anything he held in his hands when he was full of rage. I couldn't act and was immobilized. The reality is that my Mother was not immobilized and snatched the axe from Dad's hand then used it to pursue him with murderous intent.

I don't recall the exact circumstances before my decision to visit the moon. I just remember that I was lonely, fearful of Dad hurting me, and thought I would use my flying ability to escape to a safe place where Dad couldn't find me. I set off for the moon and went into interstellar space with complete awareness of my decision to do so, and with the feeling that I was physically flying through the void between the Earth and Moon.

I got halfway to the Moon and had a sense that I might get lost. The vastness of physical space that I was experiencing felt overwhelming, so I stopped and decided to return to Earth. Interstellar space that I was flying through was totally real. It was completely dark except for light reflected from the Moon as the Earth rapidly receded from me. When the Earth and the Moon were about equal size, I stopped at a point that seemed halfway between them. Space was cold, and I remember shivering. It was totally black except for the light coming from Earth and Moon. I decided at that moment to leave my soul safely in space and out of harm's way in case Dad got into another one of his rages and I became his target.

Analysis: First, let me note that to my eight year old mind, this experience was just as real as eating lunch; I didn't think about separating my physical body from my psychic self as I set off for the moon. As an eight year old, my out-of-body experiences were totally real and involved all of me.

Earlier when I was between two and three years of age and started having regular out-of-body experiences, I didn't distinguish between out-of-body experiences as just being psychic projections. I was afraid to fly high above the earth or over water in case I fell. Not knowing, that is, how I stayed above the Earth and defied gravity. The difference by the time I was eight years old was an expanded awareness of my physical surroundings and my ability to use language and name this world. However, it offered a sense of really flying, and was the same feeling as my first airplane ride.

Using my own criteria, my interstellar trip to the Moon was internal to my psyche as it violated the laws of physics. Making the assumption that a Divine Spirit exists, that a supernatural world exists, and our spirits can roam between the two, I fail.

My psyche fails, or God is a trickster. Space is not totally black and ice cold. Once we leave Earth, we are bathed in sunlight pouring endlessly through our solar system. Our side facing the Sun is bathed in trillions of photons every second and our other side is black; we are like the Moon or the Earth. Day exists on one side, and night on the other. My eight year old mind did not understand this difference, but if you are religious, you believe that an all-knowing God understands the difference. Every aspect of out-of-body projections can be explained by normal brain functions. My journey was strictly an internal affair, neurons busily firing to create an intra- psychic reality.

Conclusion: Visions that violate God's laws, the laws of physics to use Francis S. Collins metaphor in *The Language of God,* cannot be visions given to us by God. Rather, they are intra- psychic experiences of ASC.

My Genesis Trip when I went to the beginning of time and the creation of matter was planned. I knew my body was immobile as I sat in my favorite easy chair in my living room and experienced the journey to the beginning of time. I also know that this subjective experience was just as real as my trip to the moon, just as real as dying and meeting the angels, and just as real as becoming an Interstellar Giant. But, as a mature adult, I knew these experiences were in my psyche and could be explained by the same mechanisms I reveal throughout *Ghost,* and which I am now more fully developing in *Mystic.*

In *Interstellar Giant (Ghost,* 2010) I describe attempts to leave my body while interacting with my therapist. My psyche did not separate from my physical body, but instead, my physical body grew to interstellar proportions, and I occupied physical space large enough to cover half the distance to the Moon. After my Genesis Journey, I realized that instead of traveling to the   beginning of time, I could have let my physical self enlarge to fill the universe and in this fashion move to the beginning of space-time (God's dimension.)

Modern minds are not being limited by tradition. It is the capacity to control the psychic space in which we live that gives us this sense of cosmic wholeness. In either case my psyche was connecting with everything that was and is since shortly after the time of the Big Bang. This was an incredibly satisfying awareness which left me with a sense of belonging to all that is both inanimate and animate in this universe. Interstellar Giant doesn't fit into worldviews of our ancestors who envisioned Heaven as a real place above the clouds – sometimes multiple layers of Heaven at that. A Genesis Journey was beyond the historical prophets of the world who had no knowledge of the Big Bang, Inflation Theory, or physics. Modern shamans can know the difference.

Conclusion: The human psyche can experience only that which is modeled in its known physical world, or what it can cognitively create from this world. Further, cognitive creations are limited by our brain's structure and the laws of science. If you believe God is directing your vision, you know that God is not restricted by your limited knowledge or level of awareness. Restrictions of self-awareness are prescribed by flesh and blood creatures.

Conclusion: The degree to which supernatural experiences seem real to each of us does not make them real even though we become True Believers and are willing to die for them. Unless we have knowledge of the physical world through science, these episodes are explained by our psyches as actual experiences that are taking place in the world of the supernatural, God's sphere, and they are just as convincing as climbing on real icebergs.

Conclusion: Shamans and prophets become True Believers when they have experiences not common to their fellow tribal or cultural members, and subsequently accept evolving cultural explanations common to their collective world views. Historically, or today in the remaining world of primitive thought, these realities are not tested against the laws of science. As sentient beings, we are forced by our own cognitive awareness to explain what is happening to us; happily for moderns, these tests can be a fun journey into human capacity.

Evolutionary survival demands that we understand the world we inhabit in order to survive. There is nothing mystical about creating meaning as it is the basis from which we organize all of our day-to-day survival experiences. Historically we were not able to distinguish between external and internal realities as I am discussing them here, consequently, there was only one reality, and it includes primitive notions of the supernatural. This line between the natural and supernatural is not of historical origin; it is a line of modern distinction derived from science.

Aristotle's *The Nicomachean Ethics* lets us follow his reasoning as he makes real, reifies, concepts such as prudence, and discusses them not as creations from his own mind, but as realities that exist external to him. Thomas Aquinas treated Aristotle's, by contemporary standards, jumbled thoughts as being rigorous and coherent, thereby reflecting the compatibility between the two thinkers. Descartes questioned whether or not common knowledge of the world could be taken at face value. He was a skeptic. Of course it can't, as we are now aware that what seems real is often just an illusion in our minds.

The problem of what is real and what is an illusion has always been with us, and it has been considerably complicated by our brain-mind capacity to scramble neural networks (ASC). It has occupied the minds of some of our greatest thinkers. Common to such great thinkers, thinkers who have given some of us hours of delightful contemplation, is this struggle with reality. On their behalf, they did not have our modern tools to sort out empirical distinctions. *The Mind of the Mystic* makes this distinction primarily through self-experiments, but experiments that can be easily studied with modern technology. Distinguishing between the reality in our minds and that which we discover outside of ourselves has never been easy.

Conclusion: Science has often been a threat to those who dogmatize normal mystic experiences and historically made them into mansions of the mind. As we continue to reveal the origin of mystic experiences, True Believers in traditional cosmologies with worldviews based on these prophetic experiences, come to feel challenged. When worldviews dependent on realities projected from our own minds are questioned, this questioning can create an overwhelming sense of loss and conflict for committed participants. Compassion and understanding is called for as our anthropocentric world

Glen A. Just

collapses and we move beyond the historical witch hunts, torture, inquisitions, and killing of demon possessed brethren to condemnation, ostracism, and sometimes death that is still practiced in the 21st century.

OUT-OF-BODY PROJECTIONS

Two kinds of out-of-body projections are part of my personal experiences, and they are different from flying to the moon, my Genesis Journey, or simply being out-of-body in the myriad of ways we can create, direct and control. Letting my body change size is one, and the other is letting my psyche enter another living thing. Examples that I presented in *Ghost* included becoming a 6'2"giant, an Interstellar Giant, joining the North American Indian Chief as he took on the spirit of the bear, and having fun with the movie, "Ghost," where I join the hero as he passes through solid objects such as the walls of a moving subway train.

The reader will be taking note of the distinctions I make above with out-of-body experiences. As a university student, I started comparing them with the thought process of historical philosophers like Aristotle, who fail to distinguish between constructs which they create in their own minds, and something in the world external to themselves. Intellectually, as we cognitively manipulate words and ideas, and psychically as we immerse ourselves in total altered reality experiences, we fail to distinguish between creations of the mind and what exists in our external universe. We treat both worlds of subjective awareness as though each is real. Is it any wonder, then, that science fiction writers have joined historical philosophers by questioning whether this life is real, or simply a figment of God's mind, or the malevolent minds of trickster gods.

When I was going through my first divorce, I had the experience of my body rapidly expanding as I walked to the bathroom from my university office. When I entered the hallway, it was large, grey cement block, and it dominated my

12

physical presence. As I walked halfway down the hall, a rapid transformation took place almost instantaneously. I went from a psychic size of about three feet in height to my full size of 6'2" inches. I was startled by this unexpected change and how quickly it took place. I stopped immediately in the center of an otherwise empty hallway and let the experience register. Fortunately, by that time I was aware that one can experience being bigger or smaller depending on their emotional state, and the experience did not make me feel uncomfortable. It was a bit amazed though as to how quickly my psyche created a new physical me.

Abuse and neglect by both parents had given me many experiences of being different sizes when I was growing up. I remember one day spending time with my cousin in our small town of Island City. My cousin was my age and we were both about eleven. I think we were in the fifth grade. My cousin was talking about what a good fighter I was, and thought I should find some action with boys around town who were known for their fighting ability. As we walked through town with this talk passing between us, I gradually grew in size. After a few minutes, I felt bigger and stronger, and responding to the urging of my cousin, announced that I would fight the toughest town boy my age, and we set out looking for action. This childhood bravado fortunately came to nothing. (Yes, I actually felt physically larger as I mentally took on a fighting mode.)

I recall many such shape-shifting changes during my childhood; a sometimes conscious capacity that was part of who I was. My childhood psyche was a balloon that deflated with parental criticism and inflated to normal size with praise. My physical size learned to change sizes with social environments, but I did not know for many years that it could be whatever size I wanted it to be, or even that I could become an interstellar giant.

I first became aware of the ability to project myself into other bodies when I was teaching a survey course on North American Indians at Mankato State University in Minnesota. The Indian Chief in the film would take on the identity of a bear, his clan totem. The movie was wonderful, as I could feel the power of the bear as the Chief assumed its spirit. I too would join the Chief and enjoy possessing (becoming) the bear. When I entered the bear, there was a feeling of it being alive, me being alive, the two of us sharing one spirit, strength and power; unity through psychic projection.

Spirit possession is a delightful state of mind if you are doing the possessing. Spirit possession feels completely real, and we become one with the object we are possessing. It feels as real as flying to the moon or engaging in other altered reality experiences. It is not hard to imagine why preliterate people actually thought that they came to possess such spirits. It adds to my understanding of why historically people of different tribes thought the camera was capturing their souls. It helps us understand why animal-human images are so common in world cultures. (We don't need alien visitations from other worlds to explain them.)

All we have to do is change object/subject relationships around in our minds, and we are possessed by the bear, a ghost, or some other spirit. My mother taught me as a child that ghosts were real and they could possess my mind or body. I lived in fear of this possibility until I entered my teen years. The compartments of our minds, modified inter-neuronal connections, are used this way; we just change the direction of possession. We possess the bear, or it possesses us, except if it possesses us, we are often terrified and may be labeled mentally ill.

Historically, prophets such as Jesus felt this spirit possession. Jesus is reported to have taken over the spirit of Elijah when John the Baptist was beheaded, but lost Elijah's spirit on the cross.

The Catholic Church has resurrected some of the incantations to remove spirit possession in modern times, as people once more come to believe in such things. Again, I do not make light of being possessed by spirits. I never let myself be possessed by them when I was a child, but I lived in fear of the ghost getting into my body and mind. Exorcism becomes a simple set of actions once we understand the reality of being possessed, although exorcism of spirits historically takes on many forms across cultures. And it should, as all people exhibit this natural intra-psychic ability to be possessed. The exorcist works more quickly and efficiently than the therapist. However, this was an impossible discussion with psychiatrists of my acquaintance when I was a young university professor.

I became an Interstellar Giant in my mid-50s shortly after I entered therapy for the first and only time. All of my previous work had been self-therapy, but the unusual flashback to my mother smothering me in my crib was extremely upsetting. It was a memory that I had hidden in the recesses of my psyche for many decades, and it entered my awareness like a bull in a china shop.

My therapist knew from our discussions that I had left my soul somewhere in space between the Earth and the Moon and asked me get it. I had difficulty leaving my body and talking to the therapist at the same time. I had not left my body for a number of years and was feeling out of practice, so to speak. Instead of leaving my body and flying into outer space, I just grew to astronomical proportions. I realized afterwards that I could have kept growing all the way to the moon and beyond, but that was not my focus at that time.

In my 60's, I left on an out-of-body experience to the beginning of time when the universe was first created. Later when I thought of the different experiences I had with interstellar psychic travel, I realized that my Genesis Journey was equivalent to letting my physical size grow to encompass the entire universe. Both experiential realities are equally believable. My Genesis Journey subjectively connected my mind with the entire history of the universe. Thus, the feeling of belonging to a timeless something of immense proportions gave me an identity with both the animate and inanimate world in which I live.

Many people have the experience of being smaller than they actually are as the effects of abuse and trauma occur. Most are happy when they can feel normal again and regain a sense of well being. This I think is unfortunate. Letting our Self grow to a super size and experiencing the infinity of the mind is a very liberating subjective reality that brings us to a new level of awareness. It is a similar capacity that gives the alcohol, drug user, or mentally ill person intra-psychic experiences that can be either liberating or terrifying. And it is a capacity once mastered that can takes us to new levels of growth and maturity.

Our goal in life should not be one of maintenance. It should be one of growth, and if that takes us to infinity, so much the better. As Hubert Humphrey said at his son's graduation at Mankato State University back in the 1970s: "Life is not just to be lived; life is to be enjoyed."

Life is increasingly full of joy as we come to comprehend ourselves and the world and universe which we inhabit. This new world is not to be feared. We should approach new realities with an awareness that deep inside each one of us is goodness, which we can nurture and let out on demand.

2 - DREAMS

ORDINARY DREAMS

I used dream programming to conquer nightmares when I was a university student and continued this programming for about thirty-five years. I consumed available materials on dream interpretation in the 1950s in an attempt to understand my nightly horror movies. However, the chief authority at that time was Freud, and *The Interpretation of Dreams* was his bible. Rather than being helpful, Freud's work turned out to be misleading. His attempt to define dreams universally, as he also attempted to create a universal theory of personality, led him to create a Rube Goldberg theory where all dreams were sliced and diced to fit his scheme.

Freud was still the god of dream interpretation and psychoanalysis in the 1950s. I tried to follow his model, but found it unhelpful, as I will explain later. Taking a large step away from Freud's ideas, I'll first look at ordinary dreams and then nightmares using the procedure I developed to interpret and control nightmares. It's a simple model and one that readers who are unfamiliar with dream analysis should be able to follow easily and duplicate if they chose to. The model also goes beyond the cognitive-behavioral therapy that has become fairly common in the past twenty years (Pierce, 2006; Doidge, 2007).

To start, I will use an ordinary dream from last night that is still fresh in my mind (March, 2009). I reviewed the dream in detail as soon as I woke up this morning, ate breakfast and am now putting it on paper. This dream is typical of my ordinary dreams; dreams free of anxiety or negative feelings, and light years away from nightmares. First, I will review background from which the dream content comes and then show the reader how my sleeping mind put all of this material together to form an ordinary late morning dream.

My wife and I returned last week from a trip to North Vietnam and the border province in China. We created a little traveling game by seeing who could guess the ages of children and young adults who either were traveling with us or whom we met along the way. Yesterday we discussed visiting the North East China-Russia area of Russia next year. We generally visit one or more new countries annually; hence, there was nothing unusual about this conversation that would make it stand out during my dreams. Our son will be going to San Francisco to complete a joint master's degree this coming fall and we three have been talking about his visa, school, American life, and many other related things.

I also started teaching classes for the new semester this past week at a Chinese university, and was surprised during class introductions to find that one of my students, whom I had assumed was a male, was actually a female. This was unusual as I rarely make this mistake now that I have become familiar with physical differences between Chinese students from different parts of China. We have also been looking at returning permanently to the United States from China and purchasing a house. I remarked yesterday that we will need to buy a car upon returning. I sold my car three years ago when first coming to China, and I've been using a rental each summer during return visits. These are the key life subjects swirling through unorganized thoughts that represent my daily routine as an expatriate in Beijing.

My dream last night has two parts that I recall. First, I am looking at houses to buy in America, and thinking about price reductions with the depressed housing market of 2009. I am having trouble traveling in America as I no longer own a car.

But then I remember that I still have an old car stored. It is the first new car I ever owned; a 1965 red Pontiac LeMans that I wish I had actually kept. I find the car and it runs well, but needs a lot of body work. Next, I am in Russia walking through some new terrain that looks similar to areas that my wife and I have just experienced on our recent vacation to Vietnam, except in the dream I am in Russia. We are talking to a group of college students who are organizing a party for foreigners and I ask one of the young men how old he is: I guess 24, he is 28. The young man is not a student but a service worker who is helping with the party's physical arrangement. He is embarrassed by my questioning as I mistake him for a student, and he is only a service worker. We go to a dance that evening, which was arranged by the students, and find adults there ranging in age from college entrance to the elderly. The dance starts and a person I thought was a man gets up and dances with a male partner and I realize that the person is a she.

I typically drink a beer in late evening while watching the ten o'clock news. However, yesterday we forgot to order beer, which is delivered free to our campus apartment building, and I skipped this part of my routine. In my dream, I am still at the dance arranged by the Russian students and go into an adjoining room to get a beer. The room is well stocked with wines of every type and variety, but I can't find the beer. Before going to bed, I watched a TV commercial on Channel 9, CCTV, that I have seen dozens if not hundreds of times that hawks wine. I continue to search for beer but only find a different wine each time. Finally, I discover the beer half-hidden under a display of wines, and it is the usual beer that I drink when I am back in The States. At this point I wake up and review my dream for this entry, a very ordinary dream.

Where did the dream content come from? Students, traveling across an international border, beer and wine, talk about buying a house and car, starting classes with a student who at first looked like a male but was actually a female, guessing people's ages, and son getting ready to return to his university classes

Ordinary dreams have material that comes from everyday experience and is combined to create our internal movies. My dreaming mind was reviewing materials over the previous days, and when it encountered my missing beer at the Russian party, it substituted my favorite American beer. For a car, I went back to my 1965 Pontiac, a car that I still love, and brought it back to life. In one part of this dream, the Pontiac has a removable top – a feature of my first car bought in 1954, a 1949 Studebaker Champion convertible. I have also been looking at houses on the Internet, and a variety of these homes appeared in my dreams. These were homes from the Internet, not homes that I had lived in previously.

Ordinary dreams take content from one's ongoing experiences, but can also dip into the repertoire of the brain's archived thoughts and feelings. The dream and dream content above represents what my everyday life has become for a number of years; travel, teaching Chinese students, and now, making plans to return to America. My missing beer at the party in Russia became my favorite American beer. The houses appeared from my Internet search, and the reader can easily find other sources for different parts of the dreams content.

Interpretation of ordinary dreams is easy and for those who are interested it is a simple process. Start keeping a notebook by bedside and when you awake, write down everything remembered from the dream, including small segments or complete dreams. You'll soon discover the source of the dream content. Remember that your mind can access anything that it has previously recorded such as language, experiences, people, and feelings, and it can mix this content in unlimited creative ways.

We know that one's memories are dispersed in different brain centers just as other neuronal recordings are. Favorite items in my autobiographical history emerge in my dreams because they remain favorite objects of experience and recall. Time, in terms of autobiographical self, is not ordered by common weeks, months and years. Characters can be retrieved from any part of one's history, and so it goes. I suggest that interested person read Damasio's *Descartes Error* as an aid to understanding one's mind. Damasio offers the most helpful guideline that I have found for dream analysis by showing how the brain operates in close step with a model of dispersed brain functions.

Note however, that our brains create categories for everyday objects and events. Cars have neuronal boxes, or perhaps neuronal connections, in my brain, and my favorite cars still live there. There are other boxes for students and travel and this landscape of recorded memories is extensive; a quick scan of the above paragraphs gives you an idea of how we put these "objects" together in our dreams. In my experience, our mental files of information are unique to each one of us. Do not think in universal Freudian terms, but accept that your brain can record in any manner it chooses. Brains are flexible. You'll soon get the knack of sorting out your version of a 1965 LeMans from that of buying a new car. Importance equals brain salience.

For emotionally disturbing dreams, the process of interpretation is a little more complicated, but, in my experience, very different from what Freud imagined. What is universal in my dreams is not a Freudian model that says: "this dream content means..." What is universal is the dispersed multi-functionality of our working brains and memories. What is universal is the basic building blocks of thought discussed as metaphors by neural philosophers and neural scientists. What is universal is the creative construction of an autobiographical self that changes a little from moment-to-moment, day-to-day, and year-to-year.

Let's examine one more ordinary dream, but one that starts out with a strange accompanying feeling as I awake early on a workday morning, that reinforces the basic dream analysis just given. It is between 5:30 am and 6:00 am, April 23, 2009. I do not look at the clock as it would disturb my sleeping wife. Instead, I just guess at the time. This is the second night in a row that I've had this dream and the content has changed little. What has changed is my waking early, being alert, and able to recall more detail. I decide to analyze the dream and make notes as soon as I get up.

I am walking to a large auditorium to hear a speech with a group of university colleagues. My colleagues are people that I recognize from the 1970s, but the person I am most engaged with as we find a seat in the auditorium is an old lunch companion from Mankato State University. I would seek this individual out two or three times a month and discuss topics in his area of philosophy. Here was my old friend attending a lecture with me at a Chinese university in Beijing. Visually his age was the same as I last recorded it in memory.

I recognize the visual of the auditorium and it is from Winona State University where I taught between 2001 and 2006 before coming to China. This auditorium was used to greet faculty at the beginning of each new teaching year, and I last visited the site in August, 2005. Walking to the auditorium with my 1970s colleagues seemed very natural, and moving them to a new location thirty years after last contact didn't bother my dreaming mind. However, entrance to this auditorium was always preceded each year with coffee and drinks, for me, coffee, and various kinds of snacks. The atmosphere was relaxed with faculty and university staff casually entering the auditorium with drinks still in hand. This scenario was repeated in last night's dream. It was also connected with a lecture I gave last week on neural philosophy at The Graduate University Chinese Academy of Sciences.

The part of the dream that seemed strange upon awakening follows: I become aware that I am sitting in the auditorium alone and go outside to see what has happened. I see an older female family member talking to a group of women and explaining how her sales personnel are selling clothing items to fashion-conscious women, and the women customer's are being described as gullible. I recognize this family member by her flamboyant dress, something typical of her usual attire, as she liked flowers and distracting colors that tended to camouflage her excess pounds. My wife has been buying additional clothing items for the past month and tucking them away before our stateside visit. Easy explanation here, especially since my wife's Beijing sister's almost weekly purchases get discussed in considerable detail. However, I created a business for my former sister-in-law that she never owned or operated.

Another unusual twist: I realize after this brief scene that time has now slipped away again and this older family member has eaten lunch with her friends and is exiting the area across a grassy field at some distance. This is a grassy field that I often look at between classes at my current teaching position in

Beijing. I think to myself, I must have been unconscious for a considerable period of time for them to eat and leave.

Next, I look for my colleagues with whom I entered the auditorium and find that they too have eaten and are dispersing to various destinations. I follow the exiting crowd to a fence that is blocking a long table full of food. There are three people still picking up items and putting them on their plates. One of these people is a psychologist who used to work for me in treatment programs both in Minnesota and Illinois who is now teaching English in the Guandong Area of China with his wife. He tells me to take a plate before the food line closes. He is twenty-five years younger, the age when he first worked for me. This is noteworthy because we last visited two years ago here in China.

My friend's name is Bob, and I have been thinking about him over the past week and reminding myself to email him that I may be permanently leaving China and retiring stateside. One of my expatriate colleagues at the Graduate University Chinese Academy of Sciences, where I currently reside, is trying to arrange a dinner tomorrow for all foreign English teachers, and I responded by email to him yesterday. No mystery here, however, I mixed up colleagues from two Minnesota universities, added in a former friend and psychologist who is also teaching at another China location, stuck in the meal offer, and have still not answered the question as to why the lost period of time in the auditorium is still bothering me.

The fence behind which the long table of food is found initially seems to be disconnected from the rest of my dream. However, a moment's reflection, and a mind's eye review of the fence's physical characteristics, and it is identified. About two out of three nights I walk along Yu Quan Lu outside the front gate of GUCAS, traversing an area between two subway stops. At each subway station there is a new overhead walkway being erected. I have been stopping and noting construction progress at the far end before increasing my walking speed and returning home. This fence is along my Beijing walk, a fence which came down yesterday as construction progress has made it unnecessary. What better place to conceal all that food to feed

Glen A. Just

such a large crowd of university people and friends from around the world?

I have been working on Chapter Seven of this book the last few days by editing, adding content, and thinking about unconscious states that can lead to out-of-body experiences. I recognize that sitting alone in the auditorium long enough for others to eat and leave for home meant that in my dream, I was in an unconscious state for at least one-half hour or more; a normal dream connection of the "ah ha" variety.

I have been mentally reflecting about my mother's habit of using smothering to quiet her children, especially the episode that put me in the hospital and led to my death and first out-of-body experience. I had not previously spent much time thinking about the brain damage she inflicted, but have found myself putting the pieces together over the last week. I lost early speech and walking abilities, I experienced what Mother described as epileptic fits until I was at least eight years old, and I am the only member of my family that I am aware of who evidences any form of dyslexia, even though it has been fairly minimal.

I have no memory between Mother's attack on me as a crib toddler and waking in the hospital. I have clear recall of a formerly repressed memory of one of those attacks, and the next image is that of having left my body and "floating" between my father and nurse in the hospital. However, my death and meeting the angels experience approximated that of patients with asomatopsia where the sense of body frame and musculature disappears. This is a rather natural explanation for those of us experiencing these episodes, as mind and self are not suspended when this state occurs. Dad told me years after this event that he thought it was strange that Mother called him at work to tell him that I had stopped breathing. He rushed home and applied cold clothes to my head until I responded weakly, then rushed me to the hospital.

All of this occurred in a small town with a commuting time for Dad that probably didn't exceed ten minutes or so. Nevertheless, the time it took Mother to realize I was unconscious and not responding, Dad to drive to our home and apply cold compresses and then drive me to the hospital, time for the doctor to examine me, inset an IV and nose tube and pronounce me dead must have taken between a half and one hour. Conclusion: oxygen deprivation was substantial and I can only guess at the extent of brain damage. However, as a two year old, brain flexibility and dispersed neural functions obviously repaired much of the damage inflicted by Mother.

My dream waking in the auditorium at state university made me aware that a significant time period had elapsed between entering and preparing to listen to the presentation. Then, the next moment of consciousness, I find myself sitting alone with everyone gone. My brain has been processing thoughts of lapsed consciousness at a level below consciousness and the full extent of my awareness of what my brain has discovered through this process of triangulation emerged this morning. Problem solving during sleep occurs for me when I relax and my mind connects memories that it naturally keeps stored in different parts of my brain. My knowledge of my brain, and memories of dispersed functions being spread around and not localized in one center, helps me understand what is taking place in my mind and dreams.

Again, I am aware of content origin from this morning's dream. I am aware of the actors and places, I am aware that my below conscious mind is problem solving and using images that support my autobiographical self without respect to time, but with considerable respect for logical reconstruction of a "movie event" that has been the focus of my attention for some days. I do problem solve at a pre-conscious level in my dreams in a manner similar to the readers, and I can construct dream content from anything previously imaged, or images created whole within my mind. It is always fun to do so. Whether my brain is problem solving during sleep or just organizing experiences into their related "boxes" becomes apparent to me when I perform this type of analysis.

I could continue each of these analyses with a larger number of images that I can still recall upon waking this morning, but I will refrain from doing so. I think the reader can generally follow what I have outlined with the main characters, dream focus, and source of content. However, if you are a beginning practitioner of dream analysis, follow Freud's advice and write

25

down every detail that comes to mind. Do not only write down the parts that seem logical, write down everything that you can recall as though it was an act of free association. And, if you have good visual memory, you can look at much of the dream details as I have and identify content.

I am assuming that collectively we want to improve interpretations of our own dreams, and also, that some of you will go on to experiment with dream programming.

One more insight to help in this process of dream interpretation: The brain doesn't normally record all the stimuli that it encounters. For most of us, the brain efficiently repackages this information. It's similar to saving space in your computer by collapsing long files before you email them to a friend.

As we mature from the crib, for example, our mind learns to recognize the outline of mother; it doesn't need all the detail of her hair color, the mole on her left cheek, or the one tooth in front that is discolored. All the brain needs is mom's facial outline, and we recognize her. My brain does the same thing with dreams, and I think it works in a similar, if not the same way for you.   As discussed below, my mental box of cars is used over and over again in dreams, but often my brain gets creative in the process, and produces some wonderfully complex scenes and stories by combining sights, sounds, and feelings throughout my life and across all my history. Both intra-psychic and extra-psychic objects are recalled.

Analysis: Dream analysis has given me additional insights into altered reality episodes, and intra-psychic awareness from experiential experiments that I have conducted on myself provides additional insights into dream processes. For example, during waking hours, my memory doesn't record extensive details when I drive across country on secondary highways and pass through many little towns. I remember the highway's name or number and significant events that happen, but not the names and features of every little town, bridge, valley or hill, or piece of common landscape along the way.

My father, on the other hand, had almost total recall for similar drives and would start at a given point, move to the next town, comment if something caught his attention, and then move on to the next town, providing a living journey as he traveled. Sixty years after working in a small town north of Chicago, Dad once recounted all the towns along old Illinois State Highway 61 to a distance of about 100 miles as the highway passed through Chicago. I had developed a treatment program at the end of this drive, and Dad wanted to know if I drove this same highway to get there, and then he took me through his visual recall. The details in your dreams will and do vary accordingly.

As Dad recalled the details of similar drives, I could see him looking into his own mind, visually following the map that appeared there. My dreams do not have this detail and the amount of detail your dreams will have depends upon your quality of memory. Total recall is an ability most of us lack.

Secondly, I know that my mind compresses detail much as a computer software program does. In my dreams, detail associated with cars is located at consistently maintained neuronal locations, and when my dreams access these sites, any details recorded there can be combined in unique and interesting, but also functional ways to complete my dream story.

Dreaming for me is a process that efficiently accesses the files of experience that my brain has tucked away for later recall. My favorite car can return in different colors and sometimes model changes, but in my dreams, I recognize that I am fond of this car regardless of its color, working condition or model. Emotional attachment in my dream tells me this is my favorite car, even though specific features such as color or working condition may be altered. These special neuronal car files keep cars organized in my mind, and attached feelings lead to their identification. Don't forget to pay attention to these feelings, your feelings, as you practice dream analysis. Whatever was going on in your brain as it recorded images includes all of your senses: visual, muscular, auditory, somatosensory, etc.

My personality is configured such that I try to apply a logical interpretation to my thoughts – both dreaming and while awake. In the case of my 1965 LeMans, my mind recognized that I have not kept it in repair all these years, but my mind forgot that

I have not owned this car for many decades. Perhaps it is more accurate to say that when my memory recalled the LeMans and used it as dream content, time sequencing was not part of the file's content when retrieved. Thus, my need for logic recognized that the car must be aging and in need of repair. My favorite car always needs something fixed because it is now an older model. The motor works well, the tires are okay, but usually the body needs work, or the windows are broken or need replacement, and so my mind goes on.

After a few months, even if you are a beginner at dream analysis, you will come to recognize how your own unique history and life experiences are put together to create these wonderfully interactive neuronal movie files. In a year or two you should greatly improve self-understanding and have many new insights into how your mind records everyday experiences. You will also have new insights as to who you have become. You will also have taken a large step toward understanding visions.

FEELING DREAMS

I have been living a carefree life in China for the past three years, while enjoying travel and a light university teaching load. My personal history growing up as a child taught me that loneliness was something other people talked about, but not something that I experienced. I also don't get attached to geography the way normal people do. In fact, move me around the world, and I enjoy each new location for its special features, but never seem to miss the old.

For the past two or three weeks, I have been having a dream where I am back in the army, and am fully aware that I am older than the other soldiers. I am not my current age, but old enough to be the average young soldier's father. I forget which sleeping room I've been assigned to, and am not sure where I have unpacked my clothes. Drill routines are called and performed by the young soldiers, but I never make them on time. I want to eat meals, but never locate the mess hall, and think to myself that I will now need to buy food. I am constantly busy doing something for myself, and fail to notice that all the other soldiers are absent. When I ask where they are, I find them physically at a distance over strange terrain. I walk around endlessly, often hear their activity, but never locate them. I might see them at a distance, but before I can get there they have moved. This scenario has different versions, but has appeared every day or two during the middle of April, 2009, including during an afternoon nap.

Analysis: Today when I woke up from my nap, I realized the dream represents one feeling: I am lonely for my stateside family. There is no particular pattern to the dream and it does take on different forms. Rather than being in the army, I might be living in a strange place either in America or a foreign country. I can be assigned any manner of unusual job, but not work that I typically performed during my professional career. It is rare for any of my children or family to be in the dream version where I am in the army, but they do appear in the other versions of the dream, and can be any age.

After many versions of this dream, my analysis failed to find threads that would weave all the different scenarios together. Yet, there was a pattern of being in a strange place, being in a time warp and experiencing a pattern where I never get from point A to point B. When I let my search for a logical connection slip away, I was left with this strong feeling that I wished to be with my family and not where I am; a very unusual feeling for someone unfamiliar with loneliness.

Feeling dreams are like this for me. Random actions that take me nowhere, a mix of unusual people that are both familiar and unfamiliar, and goal-directed activities such as eating that never come to fruition. Logical randomness that uses any manner of memory objects means pure feeling states for me. If I let myself just focus on the feeling, it speaks to me in its own voice.

Glen A. Just

BRAIN AS MOVIE CAMERA

In *Autobiography of a Ghost,* I listed a number of insights, and will repeat most of number four with a little editing, as it provides further insight into how content gets into our dreams.

The brain can act as if it were a movie camera. I do not mean that we just use our eyesight to simply scan the world, and along with our other senses, record it. The brain can scan its own recorded landscape, which includes everything external to us as well as everything internal to our psyches. All of this landscape of the mind, some of which is created whole by the mind, can be used to create movies in our minds, and can be configured in wonderfully unique combinations. This ability permits real-to-life out-of-body experiences such as astral travel.

Dream programming is a good example of our brain's capacity to provide us with nighttime movies as we sleep. Physical smothering attacks by my mother when I was still crib confined, as well as later sexual abuse by a farmer, each created traumatizing nightmares. When I entered the University of Minnesota as an undergraduate, I was plagued by these nightmares, and brought them under control with dream programming.

I learned to substitute my own programmed dreams for nightmares, and taught my psyche to switch from nightmare to preferred dream whenever the nightmares emerged during sleep. This switching process occurred automatically while I was still asleep; the dream program auto-suggestion included this feature. I was simply using my archive of stored sights and sensations to create real-to-life, pleasing, and sometimes sensuous night movies. I taught my brain this process and used dream programming to control nightmares into my mid-fifties. After the first few months of dream programming, when I initiated the process as an undergraduate student, my dreams were modified automatically as I slept. I often became aware of this automatic process while sleeping, and sometimes consciously re-involved myself in changing the dream content.

The reader will note how easily I switch back and forth between self as subject or object.

The capacity to automatically control dreams and redirect them while I'm sleeping stays with me as I age. In fact, I am so aware of my dream processes after all these years that I would have to reprogram my Controller to eliminate this awareness and automatic sleep involvement. Dream programming offered me relief from nightmares, but I also found after weeks of viewing a specific dream-movie that I grew tired of the content. Within a few weeks of teaching myself this ability, I learned to alter the movie scripts. I created alternatives similar to movies recorded on CDs where one can change the endings or sequences through various options that are provided. I changed the dream-movies on demand; adding new segments, deleting movie sequences that became tiresome, or substituting a character with whom I had become bored with one that was new and more exciting.

For over fifty years, I have changed dream content automatically without waking. It has become a habit. However, for the past fifteen years or so, I have stopped active dream programming before I go to sleep, and I stopped before bed time programming when my last nightmare was eliminated.

Eventually I came to realize that this same capacity can be activated by a skilled guru, hypnotist, shaman or mental health worker to create experiences of astral travel, reincarnation, or false memory. In effect, the dream programming technique can be used to create and implant realities that do not exist externally to the individual. This can be done by others or by oneself, either knowingly, or at a pre-conscious level. And, as I've noted above, materials created whole in the brain are routinely treated by the brain, during sleep or during experiences of altered realities, as being true representation of our external world, just as our external world experiences, whether accurate or distorted, are treated as being real.

The "other" in all its manifestations becomes a projection of the psyche, but without conscious control by the individual, it is a reality experienced as being external to our own minds. In my dreams, the implanted realities I create are treated equally to naturally occurring external experiences. Readers who experiment with dream programming will identify this effect as they become adept at the process, or employ it in various formats such as creating altered realities.

NIGHTMARES NIGHT

My longest nightmare was initiated by smothering attacks by Mother, attacks which I recall starting with crib confinement and nursing. The source of this nightmare was implanted by Mother before I could speak, before language, during the time my mind was attaching basic metaphorical concepts such as space and time to an emerging conscious self. As an adult, and without language to represent these traumatic crib experiences, I spend years searching for their origin. Free association through language rather than using all of our senses limits discovery of traumatic events that occur in our brains in non-language areas.

Mother had a number of mental health problems, and was most probably a functioning schizophrenic with limited sexual boundaries. I recalled crib attacks when I was in therapy; attacks that had occurred more than fifty years earlier. During therapy, I gradually recalled many similar smothering episodes. That is how Mother kept her children quiet when she wanted to rest or sleep, or most likely when she was too irritated or tired to give us the attention we were demanding.

Without referencing events that I recalled in therapy, I remembered Mother smothering me when I was still nursing at her breasts, and later when she routinely left me neglected in my crib in soaking, dirty diapers. My unusual memory of nursing and being attacked in the crib means that almost all of my recall during these first two years of life is trauma centered. I attribute this life-threatening recall to experiences that came close to taking my life; experiences that I also associate with the death of two older sisters who died within six months of their birth.

Knowing that traumatic emotions are stored separately in our brains from those emotions that represent happy or pleasant feelings helps me interpret my dreams. My unusual recall of nursing at mother's breasts and being smothered at the same time represents this type of recall, as well as her attacks on me when I am still crib confined, all come from traumas that she created. This is a memory process clearly discussed in *The Emotional Brain* (LeDoux , 179-224).

The first appearance of the nightmare spawned by Mother's smothering took place in Ebe Slough, a settlement near Everett, Washington. I was between four and five years old and the news broadcasts had reported sighting a Japanese submarine in the Sound. In the nightmare, I am captured by the subs' crew, taken to their ship, and almost nightly in this dream the sailors start drilling a hole in my back to make me into a flag stand. This nightmare lasts until I am a university student and I stop it through dream programming.

I am over forty years old when I stop dream programming and the nightmare returns. In the nightmare's final expression, I am taken to the Japanese submarine and when they start drilling a hole in my back, the pressure of the drill turns into Mother's hand. I immediately identify the source of the nightmare and it stops. Whenever I identified the source of nightmares or negatively impacting dreams, my psyche automatically discontinues them. Logically, neurons connecting the two memories exchange information and the nightmare ceases to exist; the neural circuits are now open to new processing. In contemporary language, identifying the source of unwanted dreams establishes modified inter-neuronal connections in the brain between trauma and awareness. These newly created connections integrate neural pathways and remove our Controller's need to achieve unity by continuing the nightmare; to eliminate suppressed fear that is intense and has never been resolved. Unity meant that anxiety and fear in the case of my Mother smothering nightmare was eliminated, and all the psychic energy to keep this negative, crippling energy at bay was no longer needed. Expressed another way, energy used to attempt neuronal circuit closure was no longer needed.

Rationally, I knew as an adult that smothering was not something that Mother could any longer do to me. My psyche, Controller, protected me as a child by compartmentalizing these fears, thereby permitting me to nurse at her breast and function with a fragmented personality, a schizophrenic-paranoid personality according to MMPI, (Minnesota Multiphasic Personality Inventory) as I became a toddler and moved into my pre-school years. Or the possibility exists that I was young enough at age two that memories made possible by other not yet developed brain centers could not yet be retained. The lesson I learned from this specific dream analysis is that one's psyche does not distinguish time sequencing the way we do as time dependent adults. It takes any recorded feelings or experiences in the mind's archive and puts them together for a specific purpose. In this case, suppression of Mother's smothering attacks permitted me to develop from a child into an adult. The Japanese sailors substituted for Mother, and their drill was Mother's hand pressing on my back nearly hard enough to break it. Flying permitted me to enter a hidden center of my mind where I could be safe and away from harm.

Once we gain this awareness that our minds are both protecting us and suppressing materials that are too threatening, dream interpretation gets easier. The insight that the brain is constantly seeking unity of experience and stability of feelings that can be expressed in a manner that supports normal functioning came after I had used dream programming to suppress nightmares for decades. Compressing experience, much like a computer program, permits our brains to be more efficient, and this compression directs our Controller to simplify the files in our brain - unity. (Note that our sense of unity conserves energy and improves day-to-day functioning.) This process is expressed in the ethics of social relations as we age, and at its most mature level of integration, I contend, becomes the Moral Law, the final step by each of us to gain unity, and a necessary stage of individual development to create an ethical social order.

NIGHTMARES DAY

The smothering nightmare was mixed in a confused manner in my mind by my young age and the extent of Mother's criminal neglect, as well as from her physical attacks. In *Autobiography of a Ghost,* I write of being plagued by a ghost that follows me up old wooden stairs when I go to bed. Ghosts were real to Mother, and I learned from her that they actually existed, that they could haunt houses, and even get inside our bodies and take control if we were not careful. This ghost appeared before I started school, and was almost a nightly affair for many years of my youth. It would follow me up the stairs at night when I went to bed, and this pattern kept repeating in one old house after another. Its presence became most intense when I was eight years old and my father attempted to chop off my brother's head with an axe. This was a time of extreme anxiety for me, and a short time later, I traveled half-way to the moon in what was then my most long distance out-of-body experience. Death at the hands of my parents became real when Dad failed to kill my brother by one arm stroke. I created the ghost as a substitute for my fear of Mother; I made my fear into something real and concrete, something identifiable that I could deal with more rationally. The ghost was a concrete mental form of fear.

This ghost had a daytime presence. I felt it behind me when I first entered the stairway. It followed me to bed, and stood breathing over me as I cowered under the covers. The ghost disappeared for many years starting in high school, and did not return until I bought my first house in 1970 – I was thirty-four years old. I was shocked at the ghost's return as its presence was just as impactful in terms of my feeling terrified as it had been when I was a child. Decades later my feelings of fear were just as intense as when my brain first recorded them. Nightmares that come from childhood trauma such as war, earthquakes and other similar disasters remind us of this fact. From neural science we learn that traumatic memories like these can retain their strength indefinitely. I still have an instant panic reaction to loss of oxygen, smothering, and must use conscious will power to bring it under control.

The ghost left me permanently when I identified Mother's smothering hand in the Japanese flag stand nightmare, but not the associated panic response. At that time, I quickly realized the ghost was my suppressed memory of Mother coming up old wooden stairs in the house where she first taught me her unique method of child control. I never knew whether her presence would bring attack or nurturing. As the family moved frequently, the ghost moved too. How could it be otherwise? Steep wooden stairs and the ghost existed together, and the ghost returned to a similar stairway when I was thirty-four years old.

I am quite sure the reader has no difficulty following the creation of the ghost by my mind. You have followed me as I created it, you may have read my longer description of how it tormented me, and you are aware of the ghost being identified and eliminated. But do you accept the process, a process that creates endless spirits, angels, and out-of-body experiences?

I always hurried off to bed in order to get under the blankets before the ghost could catch me, or even worse, get inside my body or my mind. If I had not been fleet of foot, spirit possession would be added to my list of altered realities. Our ghosts can easily be removed by any good shaman. It doesn't matter if the shaman is a True Believer or not, but it does matter that the person possessed is a True Believer. From personal experience, these episodes produce extreme anxiety. The reality in our psyche is mixed with the brain chemistry of fear and anxiety and can be very resistant to logic and cognitive attempts at manipulation. Nightmares Night: Nightmares Day.

I want to offer some concluding thoughts to readers who have puzzled over similar experiences. The shaman, or person, who takes control of an animal like the bear or eagle is in control of the experience and knows it. The shaman knows he initiates a process that lets him become the animal, because he feels the altered reality. He doesn't need to understand what is external and what is internal, for there is only one reality - his.

When spirits are felt externally as in the case of my ghost, there are moments of fear and extreme anxiety because we know we are not in control. When spirits take control of our bodies and minds, the experience becomes overwhelming, and may be extreme enough for the individual to hide in psychosis. Dream Programming reminds us that our internal movie machine can create reality whole from our own archive of experiences. Thoughts, feelings and experiences are combined across the total landscape of what exists in our minds. There is a great sense of relief to be able to sort out the difference, and it is even more helpful when we learn to control the process.

FREUD AND DREAMS

I want to point out some of the difficulties I had with Freud's *The Interpretation of Dreams.* The book is still on the market, so I purchased another copy for review as it has been years since I initially digested its contents. Today we recognize that Freud offers many contradictions in this work; when something doesn't fit his scheme, he just adds another layer of spliced materials to bridge the gap. Frequently, this bridging mechanism is his concept of the unconscious. Similar to Aristotle, and many later philosophers, Freud created concepts, treated his own creations as being real by reifying them, and then used these word constructions to create language castles in his mind. It was a grand scheme, but it unraveled over the years. Sometimes we call these language castles models or paradigms, but they are creations internal to our brains that are projected outside of ourselves and treated as being real, a process that we come to understand more clearly by finding the origin of our altered realities, as the two have much in common. They are also speculative models, meaning they are not based on good science that can be replicated experimentally.

In *The Interpretation of Dreams,* Freud assumes that wish fulfillment is a force behind almost all of our dreams, but exempts children's dreams as being disorganized and immature. This was a problem for me when I tried to use his work when I was a university student. For example: "The dreams of little children are often simple fulfillment of wishes, and for this reason are, as compared with the dreams of adults, by no means interesting." (Brill, 38) He notes further that there are no indifferent dream stimuli except for children. He admits that he has no personal knowledge of perennial dreams, and refers to them as "so-called perennial dreams," as they represent elements that we first dream in childhood. Yet with this lack of knowledge, he has no trouble at all simplifying the learning process of children. It is not hard to understand why he had great difficulty convincing many of his patients that his interpretation was correct. He would never have convinced me, and I would have searched for another therapists.

I discovered, once I relegated Freud to the bookshelf, that his interpretations had to be incorrect. I found that dreams were not all, or even in the majority of cases, wish fulfillments, although they can be. Ordinary dreams dominate our lives when we are free of trauma. Nightmares enter when the chemistry of our primitive limbic system churns throughout the night. Fear is not just human as we can easily observe it in almost every sentient species around us from cats and dogs to mice and men. The evolutionary history of brain chemistry brings protective reactions such as fear and comes before language and more complex cognitive abilities. Let me spend a moment with my infant self in order to better connect the two.

I do not have extensive memories while in the crib or being held by Mother. My infant and toddler memories appeared when she brutalized my little body through neglect, such as diapers soaked in urine and feces drying throughout the day, hunger that accompanied this neglect, and smothering during nursing to control what was probably biting or anxious feeding. Some of these memories, such as being smothered during nursing were always with me for daily recall as I grew. The crib smothering episodes were recalled over fifty years later when I was being put through yoga-type exercises during management training, although the two acts of smothering were not of equal intensity, and did not create the same level of fear in my psyche. I can assure you that these episodes were not simple fulfillment of wishes. Why would they not be interesting to a therapist? I was both offended by Freud's interpretations and perplexed. He was the master, and I was an uneducated bumpkin from the woods of Northeastern Wisconsin seeking knowledge from similar masters. Psychiatrists of my generation were mostly Freud's bed-fellows.

Intense emotions arising out of fear, the brain struggling under chemical pressure from hyper-vigilance, anxiety and depression playing with both thoughts and primitive brain chemistry all must be considered in traumatic dreams. To his credit, Freud had no knowledge of our understanding of the modern brain. To my credit, I didn't either. I just knew that he was not providing direction and insight that made sense or was helpful to me. And, within a year, I came to know that he was incapable of even controlling his own use of tobacco – even after cancer ate his smoking tube one cell at a time. I think of Freud as a great contributor to science because he dared to ask the right questions; even though he failed methodologically.

We should not be afraid of the illogical intensity of our fears and anxieties. I learned to accept the irrational intensity of my fears and intra-psychic pain once I was able to identify my evolutionary history as a mammal, and began to appreciate the role brain chemistry plays in our thinking and dreaming moments. Self-protection through fear comes before language, the signals are chemical, and they don't disappear when we acquire language. Nevertheless, the chemical signals can be stopped by our higher cognitive processes once we identify the experiences that trigger them. We are a species that has evolved and our history remains.

In my case, I discovered interpretations of ordinary dreams when I gave up Freud. I next went to dream programming, and learned to control what became night movies. Finally, I identified how nightmares combine primitive brain chemistry with cognitive processes. Our neural pathways are not like silicon chips spitting electrons along permanent pathways. Our neural pathways operate chemically and contain the structure of our primitive ancestors. They have the ability to grow, modify, and create endless combinations of inter-neuronal connections. Primitive brain chemistry plays a critical role by expressing itself through lobes of grey matter making movies, creating nightmares, giving life variety and meaning, and creating mystics.

SHAPING THE MYSTIC MIND: TRAUMA

In *Ghost,* I detail a considerable amount of abuse and neglect during my childhood that I do not wish to repeat again.

Glen A. Just

Nevertheless, the trauma of my childhood created anxiety, depression, and what is commonly referred to as Post Traumatic Stress Syndrome. We know that abused and neglected children do not develop normal brain structures, hence, these altered structures affect how the brain responds to stimuli with brain chemistry that differs from that of normal children. The hippocampus, amygdala, and corpus collosum, for example, are reduced in size and do not function normally. This is unfortunate as they are major contributors to maintaining normal brain chemistry levels on which our emotional equilibrium is dependent. To use an analogy from the world of computers, our hardware is undersized, and critically, with enough abuse or neglect, we may be defective enough to become dysfunctional members of our communities.

One of the consequences of abuse and neglect, when it reaches critical levels, is character dysfunction and psychopathy. Individuals suffering brain hardware dysfunction, as I am referring to them, do not have their behavior corrected by making laws tougher or punishment more severe. We need early nurturing in socially stable environments and a social system that supports all children. Waiting until children are fifteen years old and incarcerating them for years or life is nothing more than an additional act of cruelty. One is not taught to love, one does not develop an integrated psyche, and one does not mature under the harsh conditions experienced by American youth in adult prisons. In despair these children lash out, become cynical, and often seek revenge. Hyper-vigilance that I know well from how my parents socialized me, does not permit maturation. It creates anxiety and depression instead.

I was a fortunate infant and child because I had a large extended family. My father was one of ten children. My father's mother, Grandmother Just, was my emotional mother when I was a child. Later, some of my aunts filled this role. Cruelty at my mother's and father's hands was compensated for by a loving extended family. This extended family of nurturing is often absent for millions of America's children. Half of my life as a child was embedded in a schizophrenic world filled with paranoia, while the other half experienced love, security and

40

acceptance. Tension between these two worlds created my story.

Children produce tens of billions of extra brain cells by the time they are three years old. As they acquire language, gain control over their physical bodies, develop emotionally, and do all the things associated with growth, the unused brain cells slip away. At age three, children have billions of active brain cells that will later become inactive. In my case, abuse started when I was nursing and still confined to my crib. I learned survival techniques in the crib such as cupping my hand over my mouth during smothering attacks by Mother; a practice that probably saved my life. Shamanic capacities such as leaving my body also began to develop during this period of time, shortly after I was old enough to leave my crib.

When I was smothered sufficiently to require hospitalization and pronounced dead by my doctor, I had to learn how to walk and talk a second time. I have no way of knowing exactly how, but undoubtedly my young brain was busy rewiring itself as speech and the ability to walk quickly returned. My first out-of-body experience occurred when I was two years old, and the ability to leave my body was something I could control at will thereafter, but it initially occurred on its own. I have been able to connect altered reality experiences from these early ages because my brain became wired in compatible configurations. I do not know, and may never know, whether or not I would have had shamanic capacities without all the trauma that I experienced as an infant and toddler.

The world of medicine is still connecting neural development to varied intra-psychic experiences. Nevertheless, mystic experiences such as spirit possession, astral travel, reincarnation, automatic writing, Zen driving and many related out-of body projections must be created through similar modified inter-neuronal connections.

I will now share my formula for mind-body control. It is the procedure that I used to conquer anxiety and depression and realize the full potential of my memory. I believe that any normal person, meaning those of us who possess normal levels of intelligence, can learn these techniques. I am not sure about individuals who have extensive brain damage and an inability to experience empathy. However, I do believe that most people who are character disordered, or pseudo-psychopaths, can learn these processes, and in this learning, they will gain greater control over their social and emotional lives.

But, first some comments about self-hypnosis, auto-suggestion, and memory. Shamans are noted for excellent memories. As a university student I extended intense study periods to eight hours without a break of any kind. As I learned this technique, my recall increased proportionately. I was recalling 98 to 99 percent of text materials with one reading; at least, my test scores supported this fact. With a follow up review, I could usually even recall all the content of footnotes and minute details. I believe that opening up additional neural pathways and connecting them to consciousness lies behind this improved memory function.

It doesn't matter that the shaman attributes his or her intra-psychic experiences to the supernatural or natural world. What is important is the newly established conscious access to an enlarged neural capacity at our conscious level.

3 - STEPS TO BECOMING A SHAMAN

OUTER SPACE: INNER SPACE

Out-of-body experiences started when I was two years old. I stopped breathing at home, was hospitalized and pronounced dead by my doctor. I left my dead body and floated between my father and the nurse, observed my motionless form lying on the bed, and moments later journeyed off to meet angels. I rejected being taken to Heaven and returned to my observation position between father and nurse. I consciously rejected death, passed through the sheets covering my corpse, reentered my body, and returned it to life. This scenario has remained a vivid memory all the days of my life. To die and not die, to leave and reenter my body, to choose Earth and not Heaven – this was my Shaman-like beginning.

No conscious part of my mind was involved in leaving my dead body, but consciousness was very much involved in my return. Out-of-body projections became a part of my childhood as I learned to fly low over the countryside, avoid lakes because I didn't know how to swim, and just enjoy the sense of freedom that came from escaping my body and the physical world. These simple excursions were the extent of my altered realities until I was somewhere between six and seven years old when nightmares combined with out-of-body flights to transported me to a Japanese submarine in the Sound near Everett, Washington.

43

When I was eight years old, I consciously set off on my first long distance journey; a journey that started with intent to sit on the moon. I stopped halfway to the moon, left my soul in space and returned to my bedroom and sleep.

Out-of-body projections that let me conquer physical space gradually matured between the ages of three and eight years. But as a child, I did not understand them, nor did I have familiarity with other states of altered realities common to mystics and religious writings. Nevertheless, when I entered the University of Minnesota and began to combine these early experiences with knowledge from psychology and other university courses, my conquest of inner space moved rapidly.

I taught myself the basics of hypnosis in my last year of high school. I found it easy to hypnotize my classmates then, but gave up the practice until I entered the University of Minnesota after three years in the army. I first used self-hypnosis to control severe anxiety and depression that was getting in the way of my studies, and was surprised at how quickly I controlled test anxiety with self-hypnosis. I don't recall the exact time lines, but I started practicing after the start of spring quarter and within a couple months, before final exams, my anxiety was under control and not interfering with test performance.

Next, I decided to use self-hypnosis to improve my memory. Removal of anxiety helped me study more efficiently, as I was often bored by basic courses or simply tired from long hours of work and study. Within a few weeks, I found that uninterrupted periods of study with total concentration on the text materials could be extended to an hour or two. Then, within one twelve week term of study, I extended my uninterrupted concentration to eight hours. I was continuously surprised at how quickly each new technique was mastered as I moved from anxiety control and depression reduction to improved concentration.

Within a year of beginning to practice these new techniques with self-hypnosis, I had achieved mastery over anxiety, depression and memory. I came to realize that the same controls could be broadened into other areas of my body and life. Next, I moved to gain total control over my body by duplicating earlier mind control techniques. Self-hypnosis was a flexible tool, free, easy to use, and seemed to offer endless possibilities. My first step to gaining total control over my body was to desensitize my hands well enough for others to stick pins in them without my feeling pain. Then I went on to control my heartbeat by making it increase or decrease at will; removing tiredness while driving to avoid falling asleep; increasing the temperature in my hands or feet by just thinking. I kept experimenting with other similar controls until I became bored with the process.

LEARNING SELF-CONTROL

I know from experience that my friends often had difficulty learning how to hypnotize others and quickly gave up the effort. In a similar manner, some people are not easy to hypnotize the first few times, and believe that it is impossible for them. Let me explore this phenomenon from an internal perspective; explaining what hypnotism and self-hypnotism feels like from the inside out. I think, however, that it is helpful if I explain using our Controller in this process. (If my use of Controller is confusing to the reader, do not worry, the concept will become clearer as we proceed).

I know when I hypnotize myself that one part of my mind enters a hypnotic state while another part observes. It's a schizophrenic sort of experience; two of me at the same time, or an I and a me that are both brought into awareness, or a world of language and the physical referential me; the process behind thought that represents both the physical and mental me. I know that some part of my mind is in conscious control as I type these letters on my computer – that part I am calling my Controller. I know that another part of my mind is regulating my blood pressure, heart beat and other automatic body functions – that part is not my conscious controller, but both parts are critical to my well-being. The "unconscious" and the conscious me are functioning as one.

If I want to control my heart beat or other automatic body functions, I have to give the conscious part of my mind permission to take control. I also know that my Controller, as I am now calling this functional part of my mind, is not in the

Glen A. Just

habit of consciously exercising this control. I have to train my Controller to perform a function that occurs naturally in some other part of my brain, a function that is performed by my autonomic nervous system. I must establish new inter-neuronal connections between these two parts of my brain – one that is conscious and one that is not normally under conscious control. In *The Feeling of What Happens,* Damasio reports an experiment by one of his laboratory's investigators using hypnosis. Pierre Rainville manipulates pain sensation and pain effect demonstrating that they are "clearly separable" (73). "Rainville has also shown that when hypnotic suggestions were aimed at pain sensation rather than at the emotions associated with pain, not only were there changes in both unpleasantness and intensity ratings, but also there were changes in S1 (the primary somatosensory cortex) and the cingulated cortex)" (73).

"In brief: hypnotic suggestions aimed at the emotions that follow pain rather than at pain sensation reduced emotion but not pain sensation and also caused functional changes in cingulated cortex only; hypnotic suggestions aimed at pain sensation reduced both pain sensation and emotion, and caused functional changes in S1 and in the cingulated cortex" (73).

I also believe that my ability to make new inter-neuronal connections is on the easy end of the human continuum. Shaman-like capacities tell me that I am a little different from the average person, but I am not a unique species. When I first experimented with self-hypnosis, the effect I got was limited. Quantifying the effect, it was slight, perhaps ten percent of what it would be in a few months. You should not expect to acquire shamanic abilities in one easy lesson. It will take practice and most likely a few months to get the hang of it all.

STEPS TO SELF-CONTROL

Steps you might follow: 1) Read a respected book on hypnosis or self-hypnosis in order to understand the process. 2) Select a common behavior that you want to master; perhaps falling asleep by the time you count to ten backwards, changing

46

the speed of your heart rate, or increasing the length of time you can concentrate on a single item, word or thought. This process can also be learned in common forms of meditation that are now widely taught around the world. Conversely, learning my routine will permit you to enjoy meditation. You are learning to focus your mind and getting rid of the clutter of thoughts that pass through it constantly. If concentration to the point of blotting out what is happening around you is easy, self-hypnosis will be easy, and vice-versa. 3) Once you have mastered simple exercises, you can go on to others that are more complex and interesting; something like my Genesis Journey where I return to the beginning of time.

In step one, I first practiced an exercise that went like this: Your hand is rising on its own, you are making no effort at all, your hand is acting on its own, you can see your fingers begin to move, it is the slightest movement, then your hand begins to rise from your lap, it has a life of its own and now begins to pull your arm into the air as well... and so on. Do not focus on raising your arm, but keep repeating to yourself that your hand is rising by itself until movement begins. Repeat this initial session for a few days until the effect feels automatic. If you cannot perform this exercise after a dozen attempts, I suggest you see an experienced hypnotist and have him or her give you the suggestion. You should allow yourself to be hypnotized and it will be helpful if the hypnotist implants the suggestion that you will now be able to perform this activity on your own. Meditation alone will not give you the capacity desired, but meditation will help you focus your concentration.

Now you are ready for step two: Practice elevating arms and legs as in step one until you are comfortable with the process and can perform it easily. You have just taught your Controller to perform an activity that you experience as taking place without your conscious control. In other words, you are establishing modified inter-neuronal connections in your brain; establishing new pathways from which non-communicating parts of your neural network become connected. This can be done in any patterns that you choose. You will begin to experience a sense of control that you've not had before. You will have awareness, if you take these steps that I did not have when I first taught myself the technique. It was an easy process for me, as I had been taught to interact with my world in a schizophrenic manner by my parents, especially my mother.

Step three simply means practice and gaining the degree of control that you desire. When you reach a stage of pain control such as being able to stick pins in your hands without pain, you have achieved a major breakthrough and the ability to block neural connections that have been functioning since you were in the womb. Not a bad level of control and one that will always be helpful as you age. A hypnotist can take you to this level of control and then transfer the ability to you through suggestion. I recommend that you try to achieve this on your own.

I have regular colonoscopies and never use any pain control medications. I just focus while I'm waiting for the doctor, and mentally put myself in the position of being the observer along with the doctor and attending nurse. I never have an anesthesiologist present, and discuss the progress of the scope as the doctor proceeds. The doctor usually says something like: "You make this look easy." I do the same with my dentist, but I must admit in my later years I use pain killers as I have actively discontinued most similar controls. When it comes to drilling in my head, it is similar to tapping on my skull and my Controller gets distracted. I could avoid pain killers and totally stop pain while in the dentist's chair, but then I would begin to separate myself from parts of humanity that I've reconnected with.

I'll give one more example of early technique development: sleeping. I approached teaching myself to relax and fall asleep quickly as a way to save lost time rolling around in bed. I started with an idea similar to counting sheep: ninety-nine, ninety-eight .... I started with a high number because I had no idea how long it would take to teach myself to relax and fall asleep with the method. Very quickly, after a half dozen attempts, I found that I was asleep after a few numbers; thereafter, I started at ten and typically fell asleep after the third or fourth count.

The time it takes you to learn self-control will depend on how well you have developed your ability to concentrate. Don't be frustrated if it takes you longer, because we are all different, but our mind-brains are built around the same neural platform.

IMPROVING CONCENTRATION

Memory, bad and good, seems to be something that we are born with. We often admire our friends and work-mates with good memories when we don't have them. I went from twenty minutes of focused concentration to eight hours of uninterrupted concentration in the time of two to three months. The ability to focus, concentrate on only what is the object of your attention, will greatly improve your recall. I didn't think of my newly gained marathon ability as being exceptional until a few years later, hence, I didn't keep track of the actual time it took to realize my full potential. I used the same process of self-hypnosis as I had used for pain and other bodily controls. There was nothing special about any one of these abilities. I just kept initiating new controls that improved my life, spirit, and efficiency. Students and professional people will find their physical limits following this procedure.

First, follow the steps to learn simple self-controls such as hand or leg levitation, heart rate, or pain. You will have trained your mind with this technique to take control of functions that your brain normally performs automatically. Now, let's train your wandering concentration to focus and block out all the other stimuli that it normally pays attention to. You can develop concentration to a point where you are only aware of one object of focus: a book, idea, mediation symbol or mood.

I started improving my twenty minute attention span by adding minutes, and I don't recall exactly how many. Time your attention span doing whatever you want to use for this exercise: I used textbooks because I had a heavy study schedule at the university. If you want to focus on one subject to practice meditation, or relieve tension, that will work just as well.

I gave myself the suggestion that I would concentrate on a specific text for a definite period of time: "You will read pages 213 to 309 without stopping; you will remember everything that you read, and at the end of page 309, you will stop and process before continuing." A simple suggestion: A suggestion that I started using after developing the ability to slip into a hypnotic state within three or four seconds. I recall that the period of concentration was focused around reading chapters from my textbooks. I had been in the habit of reading a chapter and then putting the textbook down. A practice I believe was learned in grade school and carried over to high school. This routine did not fit a university schedule which combined a full term of academic credits with a full time job.

After a few weeks of practice, I added more chapters to my study sessions and was surprised again at how quickly study time was increasing. I was able to concentrate without a break for eight hours by the end of one university term, which were quarters of twelve weeks in the 1950's. However, the first time I studied eight hours was for a mid-term exam that I had totally neglected. The routine encompassed reading and memorizing half of a textbook. When I finished reading and put down the book, neuronal fireworks exploded in my brain. I was shocked by this effect as it felt as though a blood vessel had burst. I discontinued these longer sessions shortly after that, and found it helpful to take breaks for liquids and snacks after four hours. You will want to experiment with your own level of physical endurance, as it will be associated with your age and physical condition.

Improved concentration has stayed with me life-long. Further, as the length of my ability to concentrate improved, so did my recall. I always had good recall, but only for short lessons. Recall isn't very good when our minds wander after twenty minutes or so. I typically recalled 98 percent or more of new text materials after one reading, and if I studied the material twice, it was unusual for me to miss any test questions on class exams even when footnotes were included. My spouses became irritated with me when I was reading as I blocked out everything else, including their attempts at conversation. Once you develop these techniques, you will keep them forever as they are self-reinforcing. You will also be exercising your brain and keeping senility at bay. You won't need Merzenich.

ZEN DRIVING

In *Autobiography of a Ghost* I recount experiences of Zen driving, out-of-body projections with the Ghost in the movie "Ghost," and a film where a shaman of America's Northwest Coast takes on the spirit of the bear. When the reader develops the ability to leave his or her body consciously, there is much fun to be had with this technique. If you are familiar with religious or mystic experience, you are also familiar with numerous stories, either first or second hand stories, that recount these experiences of ASC by shamans and prophets. If you enjoy astral travel or experiences of reincarnation, you will notice the similarity. In fact, you won't be able to tell them apart. In either case of mystic reality, practicing or not practicing experiences of altered reality, you can come to gain conscious control over the process and add a new chapter to your inner life.

Let's assume that you are now a practitioner of self-hypnosis and can control your heartbeat, blood pressure, and pain. Further, you have taken the next step and extended your concentration. But, you have not yet practiced out-of-body trips.

Many readers will have experienced out-of-body trips without any of this other stuff coming first. Out-of-body trips or being possessed by spirits is an experience not uncommon with alcohol and drug users during psychotic episodes, after physical trauma, during sickness, or in rare cases to my knowledge, spontaneously. Again, let us look at these experiences from the inside out.

By age three, I was leaving my body regularly as it was a delightful psychic experience to fly low over the countryside. When I was out flying, however, it felt as though my physical body was attached, and the intra-psychic reality made me fearful of flying high or over water. Out-of-body experiences of this nature are totally real. My first experience where I consciously leave my body during a normal work environment occurred with the shaman movie where the Indian becomes the bear. As I watched the shaman on film gradually assume the identity of the bear, I could feel him entering the bear and the

51

two becoming one. I didn't just see these actions taking place on film; I experienced the transformation in my own mind. This was an easy step for me, as my psyche had been experiencing out-of-body trips for years, and made these inter-neuronal shifts almost without effort.

I enter the bear with the shaman and become the bear – a human-bear persona with human consciousness and bear-like strength and size. My physically projected self grew in size as well as it was taking on the characteristics of the huge bear. How else could it be? So, what was taking place in my brain and my mind during this transformation? Previously established inter-neuronal connections that I don't use every day came back into play. My mind, soul, or spirit, as you will, separated from my physical body. I didn't just leave my physical body; I left my body and entered that of another – the bear. Did I possess the bear or did the bear possess me? My perception of the shaman's transformation as he became the bear was shared with him as I merged with the bear's identity. Physically in my mind I was a new entity, a humanly conscious bear.

In reverse, I believed my mother as a child. "Ghosts can enter your body and take control of your mind," she taught me. I lived in fear of the ghost that followed me for years as I accepted this belief as a child.

Now let's think about what's happening as we enter the bear's body and take control. We are experiencing separation from our physical bodies and exercising or modifying new inter-neuronal connections. The sensations are real, but we know what we have done and are in control.

The shaman has entered a mystic state of altered reality, and in his traditional culture he is observed becoming the bear. I have entered a similar state, but one that I control, and with modern knowledge of how my mind works, the experience is not mystical at all – it is fun, and one that can be repeated endlessly. Whether one is aware of their intra-psychic control or not doesn't matter, for the experience is totally real. In one situation you are a True Believer, and in the other, a psychic adventurer.

Let us reverse the direction of control and confront my childhood fear of ghost possession. I kept the ghost at bay by running up steep wooden stairs to my bedroom, jumping into bed, and covering myself with blankets. Physically, I engaged in acts to keep me separated from the ghost. I taught myself a routine similar to the steps used for self-hypnosis; steps that gave me control over the ghost and prevented the ghost from possessing my body or mind. If I had let the ghost slip partly into my body or mind one time, it would have been easier for him to slip in further the next time. When we are possessed by spirits, our brains have modified their inter-neuronal connections and the experience is both real and terrifying. An experienced shaman or priest can follow a reverse-type of hypnotic suggestion and remove the spirit. In days of old, the reality of suggestion was shared by both the priest and the victim, or by contemporary practitioners of voodoo.

In various types of psychosis, loss of control is experienced when daytime movies appear without any effort on our part; visions from the neural network of dreams that are equally real and vivid. We hear voices that are not there, voices that no one else hears, but are equally real and vivid. We have feelings of deep sadness when there is nothing special to be sad about, or something we wish to forget is not forgotten, but the feelings are overwhelmingly real and cannot be removed. I suggest that medical practitioners and therapists should study how we alter our inter-psychic neural patterns to better understand both psychosis and altered realities. I am quite sure that many aspects of poor mental health can be eliminated simply using these techniques, as I eliminated them from my own mind this way.

UNITY AND HEALTH

A few months after entering the University of Minnesota, I was given a Minnesota Multiphasic Personality Inventory (MMPI) when I was twenty-one years old. This personality test measures deviations from normal, healthy personalities. I had three major elevations that put me into critical ranges: paranoid-schizophrenic, obsessive-compulsive, and psychopathic. In truth, I was suffering from a severe case of post traumatic stress syndrome from parental abuse and neglect, but I did not understand this syndrome at that time.

Retrospectively, I can now ask what was going on in my brain. Behavioral indices are compatible with my mother having a schizoid personality. The world of ghosts and spirits was real to her. She had a public life as a dutiful and concerned mother, but other times, she smothered her children and neglected them feloniously. My father was a functioning alcoholic prone to outbursts of rage, who had an immature, selfish and self-serving personality. He was a womanizer and as much of a pretender of good parenting as my mother was. Two of my sisters died in infancy from what our family doctor later described to me as "neglect." I almost became Mother's third victim and not only was I declared dead by our family doctor, but experienced death and a beginning trip to Heaven where I met angels. This was my world as I passed through childhood carrying the heads of parental monsters in both arms.

My steps to health included the use of self-hypnosis as I've outlined earlier. Intra-psychically my fragmented personality with critical elevations on the MMPI was gradually being transformed as I overcame one obstacle after another: anxiety, depression, a violent temper, and lack of concentration. In all this process, over about two years, I not only stabilized the chemistry in my brain to eliminate mood swings and anger, but also increased my sense of well being and unity.

These were my first lessons on becoming whole. These lessons taught me to do whatever I wanted to with both my body and mind, created an historical perspective that unity meant freeing one's mind of compartmentalized contradictions, and lessons that, in historical context, let me understand the plasticity of my own brain and how it could be developed and controlled.

Maturity, thy name is unity; maturity, thy name is equilibrium. Maturity's middle name comes from integrating and cleansing the separate boxes of trash inherited in our childhood.

4 - MORAL LAW

MORALITY IN THE FLESH

The moral law is pervasive in our lives, across all cultures and peoples and throughout known history. Therefore, it must come from the Divine if one is a theist, or it must be in our genes if one is a non-theist - agnostic or atheist. Universality does not make the moral law or any other common human behavior automatically originate from God. How can we answer this question: "What is the source of the Moral Law?" Reading endless tracts of religious literature leads some to conclude that the moral law must be of Divine origin. The question of origin is always asked the same way – God or nature – thus, the answer naturally follows. The clarity and logic of a C. S. Lewis for the moral law coming from God is most appealing, but clarity of thought does not provide infallible conclusive logic. Each generation knows its own clarity as does every religion; clarity that comes from tradition.

I have enjoyed Francis Collins book *The Language of God* for its directness, good use of logic and reasoning, and for his ability to search deeply within himself, and when doing his most honest search, share his conclusions with his readers. Sincerity and self-honesty are indispensible in any search for the truth, and Collins meets this standard in my opinion. However, he relies on our old favorites: universality of right and wrong is found across all cultures and history, therefore, it must have a Divine origin.

He says that "… humans are unique in ways that defy evolutionary explanations and points to our spiritual nature. This includes the existence of the moral law and the search for God that characterizes all human cultures throughout history." (Collins: 204) Truth would be so easily determined if universality of cultural practices explained its origin. It does not! War has been just as universal as our search for God, or the universal existence of the moral law in all cultures. If universality makes something true, then we should also argue that God wishes us to kill each other because he has made war part of His Divine Order, a Divine Order that is found throughout history and across all cultures. Is this a rational thought process, or a repackaging of old ideas?

Collins states: 1) "The second objection from the Dawkins school of evolutionary atheism is another straw man: that religion is antirational." Collins takes Dawkins to task for not adequately describing the faith of serious believers throughout history. "Dawkins definition of faith is "blind trust" in the absence of evidence, even in the teeth of evidence." Collins sees serious believers such as Augustine, Aquinas, and C. S. Lewis as going beyond blind trust (Collins, 164) Collins goes on referencing Dawkins and Dennett: 2) "… an acceptance of evolution in biology requires an acceptance of atheism in theology." (Collins, 161) Here I must side with Collins and agree that Dawkins and Dennett are both stepping beyond the limits of logic.

Neither Dawkins nor Dennett can explain how the universe became so finely tuned as to permit the emergence of life, and what appears to be an inevitable consequence of life's emergence – evolution. We are close to creating life from scratch in the laboratory, but doing so will still not answer the question of why the universe is so fined tuned as to permit life, even as we approach deriving life from the test tube. We are compelled to answer how this fine tuning is possible before we can state absolutely that it is God or not God. Collins accepts that we understand the DNA code, and he sees this code as God's handy work. Understanding life as we learn to create it in the test tube will be no different; it will still be God's handiwork for the theist, and nature's blind creation for the atheist. For Collins, it will just be another process we understand that is similar to evolution itself.

To assume that the universe occurred by accident and we were just lucky enough to get finely tuned equations of physics to make life possible, and then tell the reader this must be accepted at face value because it is logical, seems to leave the writer of this idea in a process of circular reasoning. The universe is fined tuned, thus we have life: We have life because the universe is fine tuned. And, if Dawkins is successful in charging Collins with "blind trust," he must be tarred with the same brush. I find Dawkins to be an excellent writer, and I thoroughly enjoy his arguments, but the fact that his books sell well is not proof that his logic is infallible any more than cultural universality makes the moral law a given from God, or anymore than evolution comes from blind nature, therefore, nature can only exist by accident, and God does not exist. Interpretation? Interpretation: The endless arguments of True Believers – either atheistic or theistic True Believers.

Collins and I apparently both enjoyed Hawking's *A Brief History of Time.* Hawking expresses the sentiment that the possibility of getting such a fine tuned universe is enormous. It is difficult not to appreciate Hawking's position when we realize that the slightest modification of fine tuning after the Big Bang would have made the emergence of life impossible. Most of us, when we see such enormous probabilities written into nature, come away with greater awe of our special place in evolution.

In the course of human history, nature's answers to the questions asked by humans are gradually answered. Disease is caused by organisms not spirits; the Earth rotates, not the Heavens; fusion drives the Sun, not the Sun god. I am arguing that we do not find answers in "logic's historical moment" no matter how appealing that temporary logic is at a particular point in history. We find answers by testing hypotheses, being able to duplicate our research findings, and creating verifiable theory based on this process. Theory is not speculation about what is; theory is the ability to duplicate research findings, support or disprove our assumptions, and thereby create a standard body of knowledge, as is the case with evolution. But the practice of science has not answered the question of ultimate or primary causation.

I believe unequivocally that the moral law comes from our own psyches. It is an expression of consciousness that originates in our DNA. It is either part of nature's plan or God's plan depending on your worldview, but it is integral to the structure of our brains and the minds that come from this structure. If you are a theist of the Collins variety, nature's plan is God's plan, and there is no conflict between the two – a comfortable place to land in this world of jumbled ideas. We do not answer the question of how to cure sickness by arguing that our understanding of disease must be correct because contemporary knowledge supports our position, as was the case before science was applied. Aspirin's ingredients worked for decades before we understood how it worked, but that did not keep tribal people from using it, or claiming that it was a special gift from God. Partial knowledge is not the final answer because we wish it to be. We must demonstrate why and how our assumptions are correct and verifiable through research, or admit speculation and continue to search.

To say that the moral code is beyond research and belongs to the realm of God, or that the moral code exists because it is part of nature, is to state a position based on belief, not fact. Either position fails to ask the question correctly. How does the moral law come into being? We should not phrase the question as being either true or false – is the moral law from God, or is it from nature? I believe better questions are: How does the moral law come into being? Is the moral law built into our DNA? Are there other sentient animals on this planet that exhibit the moral law? Under what conditions is the moral law expressed or not expressed when the organism demonstrates this innate capacity?

In *Autobiography of a Ghost,* and with further elaboration in *Mystic,* I explain how the moral law emerges from a healthy psyche that it is part of mature brain functioning and an inevitable part of an integrated mind. I have followed my own development along this line carefully and challenge critics to refine this interpretation or find a better alternative. I also believe a more comprehensive explanation will eventually come from neural science and psychology. The process to maturity, the process to integrating a fragmented self, leads us through the following stages: 1) brain chemistry is stabilized when our past traumatic childhood is brought under control, 2) fragmented interaction with our physical and social environment is overcome as our relationships with others become stable and predictable, 3) different levels of maturity are realized as stable brain chemistry and improved social relationships are achieved, thereby removing ongoing states of anxiety, depression, and hyper-vigilance that have been doing two things to our physical brain: a) poisoning our brains with its own chemicals, and b) keeping our inter-neuronal networks from efficiently serving us. I will say more about neural development later, but note that the constant surge of flight or fight neuro-transmitters stops our maturation. (I also outline this developmental process in considerable detail in *Ghost*).

The moral code comes from our psyche and is grounded in integrated brain functions. If the brain is not permitted to develop normally, the moral code does not emerge, as is the case with psychopathic personalities, or it is weakly developed. For example, about half of the people tested with psychopathic personalities in prison grow out of the condition as they approach their fourth decade. These individuals are often defined as not being true psychopaths. A funny way, I think, to conduct diagnoses. One time you see it, and the next time you don't. If the condition continues, it is a correct diagnosis, and we have a "true" psychopath. If the condition goes away, the diagnosis is still correct, and we have a "false" psychopath. Clearly, an explanation for this transition from "true" to "false" is required. And, I think the explanation is easily found: stabilizing brain chemistry, and strengthening or modifying inter-neuronal connections that occur when the individual's environment is stabilized, permits brain maturation to continue. That is, as long as the brain structures themselves are fully expressed.

Glen A. Just

PRISONERS AND PSYCHOPATHS

Lynn Picknett talks about imprisoned criminals finding God and becoming good citizens. However, when we do controlled experiments, as has been the case in the Oregon Prison System, we do not find less recidivism for the converted prisoners than we do for those who have not been converted. Picknett helps perpetuate an idea that is popular through this commonly accepted myth: wide-spread assumption of God's direct intervention does not make it true, any more than wide acceptance of a religious belief means that it must come from God. What is going on in the brain and mind of criminals that makes them so resistant to the moral law? The explanation is easily found in my own experience: stabilizing brain chemistry and strengthening or modifying inter-neuronal connections. However, in the case of those labeled as True Psychopaths, when this syndrome continues, modification does not occur, and the brain appears damaged beyond repair.

My argument for the moral code being internal to our psyches is strengthened by our awareness of psychopathy. Brains that are too severely damaged cannot be repaired, and the person with a crippled brain remains a burden and a threat to society. If God were working directly to modify damaged brains, then devotion and prayer should do the trick. It does not. Prayer and church attendance in prison does not appreciably improve recidivism when the prisoner is released. However, it does provide a quieter, more easily controlled prison environment by keeping prisoners busy and positively occupied. The main role of clergy in prison is providing support for depression, and loneliness, and to combat despair. And God bless them for this act of kindness and faith in humanity. In my experience, they are some of our most dedicated and humane prison personnel.

Prisoners who are in stable environments often comment after years of confinement that they no longer recognize the person who was initially imprisoned for their heinous crimes. They talk of their former selves as if they were referring to someone they met years ago. And, in one sense this is true. I have personally known hundreds of ex-offenders and worked with even more in the corrections system, and many of these individuals have become new persons. Some I have known have gone on to repent through social action, providing endless support to other offenders released from prison, or becoming model citizens in their community by supporting a multitude of noble causes.

Let me compare contemporary thinking about punishment law and what it means to real people. Punishment of young offenders that puts them in prison stops their maturation. Young prisoners are victims of understaffed prisons across America, and they live in a constant state of fear and hyper-vigilance. Their minds are subject to stresses similar to soldiers in war. Emotional growth is stopped by the toxicity of their own brains, and typically they regress in terms of the moral code. Those who believe in this type of punishment are neither students of science nor of morality. They are perpetrators of barbarism and destroyers of the common good. Damaged psyches do not experience the moral law. It is not permitted to grow into concern for others. Pressure cooker prisons do not permit the growth of conscience and greater identification with one's fellow human beings.

Damaged psyches in prison degenerate even further into the well of human hate and despair as is evidenced by the increased rate of violent crimes committed by these young offenders upon release. It would be so simple if prayer solved this problem for us, but it does not. It would be so simple if punishment improved morality, but it does not. It would be so simple if God in his wisdom would enter our prisons and demonstrate his skill as a brain surgeon. He does not. If you are a theist, God gives us our DNA and all its potential, but I believe we are responsible for the results. If you are an atheist, nature gives us our DNA and all its potential, and I still believe we are responsible for the results. There is no conflict here. So, why does the stupidity of prison barbarity continue?

As the world's atheists and theists continue to beat upon each other with ever hotter breaths, the minds and souls of youth are pushed into a sub-human realm of fear, hate, and isolation. I cannot see any way out of this dilemma unless we take responsibility for our true nature, our nature as revealed by science, not the supposed nature of humanity expressed by the world's false dogmas. God within or nature within leaves us with the same commitments to each other, which are ones that demand rationality.

CONSCIENCE

As with persons committing heinous acts of cruelty against one another, whether these acts are committed in the name of God or greed, we are appalled at the lack of morality in war and on the street. Conscience operates at its highest level when the brain is nurtured in infancy and childhood. It does not function well when levels of brain toxicity exceed a basic threshold. Conscience seems not to exist when the fragmented self struggles in ignorance to survive day-to-day. Reducing fragmented, warped if you will, personalities requires environments free of fear, long-term caring relationships from those around us, and removal of the social predators that support this environment.

The worst kind of social predator that I have encountered in a lifetime of working in, around, and through the correctional system of America is the individual who denies supportive conditions to children, as in Minnesota Governor Pawlenty's, "share the pain, budget cuts are necessary, we will correct the problem later, or, it's a problem of morality, not funding."

Empathy is our ability to place ourselves in the position of another, and to experience what is happening to this other person emotionally, physically or spiritually. It is a short out-of-body trip if you will, and when accompanied by tears, it is known as sympathy. This intra-psychic ability to become someone else in feeling and thought at any given moment is lacking for those without conscience. Understanding psychopathy is difficult, as it takes considerable effort and time because the syndrome is so alien to the normally socialized individual.

Doctor level therapists in prison are constantly being manipulated by prisoners without conscience even though they have studied psychopaths extensively. Realities that exceed the limits of our emotional capacity, the experiential limits of our own minds, are most difficult to comprehend. In reverse fashion, normal people remain an enigma to the psychopath. Popular movies like "Silence of the Lambs" titillates the viewer with extreme behaviors of which the psychopath is capable, but these movies do not improve our understanding of the condition. These movies do, however, increase our fear and hatred as they make large sums of money for a select few. The modern equivalent of the Roman Coliseum becomes ever more gruesome and bloody.

After years of experience with individuals suffering from similar developmental deficiencies, I can state with a considerable degree of certainty that recovering, or pseudo-psychopaths must undergo modified inter-neuronal connections for a conscience to mature or emerge. Prayer books do not do it, unconditional love does not do it, and churchgoing does not do it. If I amputate one of your legs and then incarcerate you until you can win the hundred yard dash, you will think of me as cruel, crazy and bizarre. Yet how many politicians have been elected by proposing this same one-legged punishment policy? Run the race or else, and commit offenders for ever longer periods of incarceration.

Group homes for children and young adults are little better than prisons when they fail to provide conditions that stabilize brain chemistry, when they fail to provide safe environments through total therapeutic community living, and when they ignore other developmental needs of children. Social work and mental health interventions based on "love 'em to death" are not effective. Effective therapy must meet the critical conditions I have been describing. The blind lead the blind through ego, inadequate education, or greed by claiming that salvation is found in one pet therapeutic model or another, one favorite university department or another, or one special religious door to Heaven. Children must be able to live without fear and experience an environment conducive to normal brain development, or there is no door to Heaven.

I will say more about overcoming schizophrenia later, but note the similarity between the brain of the psychopath and that of the schizophrenic. Something has gone wrong with the hardware in the computer-like, inter-neuronal connections in his or her brain. We cannot run superior software called the moral law on a hard drive designed for 16 K.

Let me add a note about good prisons and good group treatment programs for offenders. We do know the difference between them, but we rarely use this knowledge.

If the inmate is provided a secure environment free of fear and predation, he or she can continue to mature, but this is rare in America. Prison administration or guards who permit sexual assaults, physical intimidation, or provide a pressure cooker environment to torture inmates are not only being inhumane, but must claim allegiance with the dark forces of nature. First, we must commit to good prisons or continue to drain our treasuries by incarcerating millions for life. Unreasonable, perhaps foolish, ungodly, vile, stupid – you can choose your favorite word – all violate the human conditions necessary for growth.

Therapeutic communities that are real therapeutic communities and not just labels pasted on for promotional purposes, which by the way are few and far between if we are to believe the meta-analyses, provide stable environments for personal growth.

The bedrock condition necessary for all effective programs is safety. Secondly, the development of trust in each other and staff, which is not possible unless the client feels safe, and thirdly, a supportive program that is expressed from the time one rises in the morning until one goes to bed at night. It is rare to find such programs in America for youth that are severely damaged.

Other qualities of successful treatment programs are easily teased from the growing number of meta-analyses that are available over the past quarter century. Effective treatment programs provide the client with easily understood explanations for good behavior and provide support for model behavior that the clients accept in a language that they understand and with a consistency across disciplines such as family therapy, cognitive therapy, sex therapy, and the like. For instance, meaningful family therapy cannot use an esoteric treatment language different from other types of therapy when the client only understands one of them.

SISTER THERAPIST: BROTHER GURU

Treatment is effective within group settings or individually when the above conditions are met, but they are rarely found for those with severe behavioral disorders, because the public supports harsh treatment and incarceration. Public anger drives inmate hatred. Altered realities, whether they are out-of-body, cruel acts of a gang, or psychotic episodes, are most effectively corrected when there is compatibility between the individual and the messages he receives from his helpers. Therapy is most effective when conducted under circumstances that I have referenced above, or in true therapeutic communities. Always, conditions that destabilize brain chemistry must be eliminated, and in their place, assured safe environments with a common therapeutic language must be provided.

Religious conversion for normal, but seeking, personalities follows a pathway similar to treatment for the behaviorally disordered. The clergy or guru explains a worldview that is accepted by the convert, and in this acceptance, the convert experiences a new sense of knowing and understanding what has happened to him or her, and feels that a burden has been lifted. If the conversion is accompanied by an altered reality experience, it is even more effective, as with alcohol and drug addicts. Acceptance of a comprehensive worldview quiets the fragmented brain, stress is reduced, and brain chemistry stabilized. Anxiety and depression will be either controlled or reduced, and the convert will express satisfaction with his or her new identity – even to the point of feeling born again, and new social relationships are established that support stability in the individual's life.

The difference between the religious convert in the community and the prison inmate is the degree to which the two have acted out behaviorally. However, as a growing body of research indicates, piety or good behavior does not follow unless social and emotional maturity is also nurtured.

We cannot imagine ourselves undergoing therapy with someone whom we disagree with or dislike. Therapists and clients share this compatibility or the client is referred to another mental health worker. If I love my therapist, I tell others; if I love my religion, I tell others; if my therapist or my religion improves my life, I am a believer. The tune is different, but the music is the same. And for individuals who convert from one religion to another, or for clients who become addicted to therapy and have a lot of money, each becomes a True Believer of the moment. Serial converts who move from one social cause to another share this rush of emotional unity, share the quietude of the moment that comes from conversion bliss, share the magical chemicals released in their brains that brings contentment to their souls, and then move on to their next fix.

I am not poking fun of those who love conversion and are usually its strongest advocates. I am asking the reader to look inside the brain and understand. Their conversion is not maintained by logic or dogma. Their well-being and sense of belonging or connecting emerges when newly integrated and previously fragmented psyches achieve cognitive focus and peace, even if it is temporary, by stabilizing their brain chemistry and giving them a sense of purpose and meaning. The incurable proselytizer becomes addicted to the chemical rush in his or her own brain. Perhaps this is a different understanding of disciples.

The shaman historically, whether the chief becoming the bear, or a religious healer bringing relief to the sick, is able to create an effect in the witness that is experienced as being totally real. It may or it may not last, but for the moment it is a "rush." It is a force that can bind us unto death, or it can be an instrument of war. It can be a life-long love that provides a sense of everlasting joy and euphoria. It is a force cynically used by the usurper of our money. It is a bond that builds congregations, and it is the glue that makes therapy work. And since in its absence there is despair, it can be life itself.

DELIVERANCE

The moral law is common to all humanity because it is part of the normal brain's potential. It is in our DNA, and it is an internal brain emergent when love and caring prevail. It is the basis of Heaven and Hell, and in its absence or presence, it is both the light and dark force within humanity. It is too close for us to see and can only be felt when we learn how to experience it inside our own minds. Those who see will be saved. The blind will not see, so Jesus says don't waste your time with them. The gates to Heaven are within, and so the story goes. I am saying: we can do much better than this.

The Moral Law may be violated when we define others as being outside of our own group, and group membership may be used as an excuse to kill or exterminate others as in the Old Testament. The Moral Law cannot be violated once we individually learn that its source is internal to our own psyche, and once we understand that all humankind is built from the same DNA. We cannot say only my village, only my state, only my nation, but must come to acknowledge the common capacity within our species. Paraphrasing one of our great prophets, truly I say unto you, no one shall know the Kingdom of God unless they come to the truth.

There is no conflict between the theist and the atheist on this point. All that remains is the question as to whether this condition we share across humanity is God-given or a blind act of chance. Quoting Lynn Picknett: "The truth shall set you free." And further, "Free of priests, gurus and dogma, the progress of our spirit is – perhaps frighteningly – nothing more or less than our own responsibility. After years of making God in our own image, perhaps it is appropriate to allow him/her to return the favor, but this time from the inside out." (243)

I enjoyed Spinoza, when I discovered him through my army buddies, for his abstract concept of a timeless God who resided within each of us. This was a feeling state that I inherited from early childhood experiences of altered reality. Spinoza ran into trouble with the church because his internal God implied that the soul was perishable in the sense that each one of us has a self-soul that stops being at death. Of course, this is a huge violation of dogma for Christians and Jews. However, the soul as a timeless entity created and recreated endlessly also has another meaning. It is a timeless expression of life's evolution that makes perfection possible. It evolves, but not by reincarnation; it evolves through genetic and social maturation.

Damasio says that "nature lacks a plan for human flourishing, but nature's humans are allowed to devise such a plan." (Spinoza in Damasio, 1999, 280) Again I must disagree with one of my favorite neural scientists. As we watch the progression of consciousness emerge in other species from dolphins to bats, it is almost impossible not to appreciate the encoding offered by nature's DNA. We not only have consciousness, but an awareness of our own consciousness. What, then, is the next step in evolution? Is it the ability of self-conscious beings such as ourselves being able to create a social structure upon which universal social harmony comes into being?

We have this vision which is often expressed in various musings about utopia. Our earliest visions being those of Heaven, however, our self-responsible vision is now predicated on using the intelligence of an Intelligent Universe to make this vision a reality. The bright side of religion or atheism means that we accept the hand of God or nature that is working through us. There is no conflict here in terms of our collective efforts to achieve "goodness." The conflict may be with primary causes for the atheist, but it cannot be with fostering the moral order itself. For theists this is God's domain, not yours or mine. Religion can only meet the test of the Moral Law by making a commitment to nurture the growth of good within, regardless of how primary cause is interpreted. Common ground is not a bad place to start for the creation of a harmonious world.

5 - MYSTICS AND MYSTICISM

IN THE BEGINNING

I have provided an explanation for the Moral Law as a natural expression of a mature psyche, and demonstrated the origin of historical and world-wide religious experiences as these altered realities emerge from somewhat unusual but normal brain functions. This does not answer the ultimate question of how the evolutionary sequence leading to our brain's structure was set in motion, whether by God or a blind act of evolution, but it does explain the universality of mystic experiences such as shamanic spirit possession, out-of-body projections, astral travel, speaking in tongues, reincarnation, and why spirits/angels are universal to the human condition. Opening or modifying the right inter-neuronal connections in our brains creates these varied altered realities. The experiences are magical and often leave us with an experience atypical of normal neural networking. Nevertheless, when we learn how to create, control, and direct these experiences, it becomes obvious that the phenomena are internal to our brains.

Understanding the universality of our basic human capacity to create altered reality, experiences that have historically been understood as coming from the Divine, begs examination of the multitude of these explanations world-wide. It is undeniable that this capacity is universally in our psyches, even if it is unusual, when we consciously learn how to leave our bodies, enjoy the fun of speaking in tongues, automatic writing, or experience the reality of a former life. It is not the variety of world-wide and historical interpretations that is critical. (One can enjoy religious literature and anthropological studies as an appreciation of the variety of cultural interpretations involved). What begs understanding is how our brains create such true-to-life experiences of the mystical. It is natural and inevitable that we search for their source. The primitive psyche finds the source of these experiences to be out somewhere beyond our bodies and minds. Universally, that is how we feel, while at the same time leaving us with the certainty of knowing that these experiences are coming from outside our minds and bodies. After all, dying for one's beliefs doesn't happen because one has doubts.

I have demonstrated in *Autobiography of a Ghost* and now in *Mind of the Mystic* that shamans, prophets, and major religious figures throughout history have been using this capacity. Some unquestionably were True Believers, and others, as we know them in modern society, charlatans. We come to explore these phenomena from a different point of view as neural science and developmental psychology increasingly explain what is happening in our brains.

I can assure the reader, who has not yet developed the ability to enjoy altered reality experiences, that awareness of the process does not destroy the reality effect. How could awareness destroy the reality effect? We experience altered reality through total involvement of our senses, and total involvement of our senses is how each of us creates reality day-to-day, moment-to-moment. Nothing strange here!

INHERENT NEED TO WORSHIP

I visited a major Buddhist site in Beijing this past year, 2008, and accidentally stumbled on a ceremony for new converts. The square was filled with a multitude of people, perhaps a couple thousand as they spilled around fountains, pillars, and each other; wall-to-wall people embracing Buddha with the fervor of Muslims prostrate at Mecca, or the total commitment of born-again Christians; an impressive sight in a country claiming atheism as its religion. Political systems are not able to remove the certainty that comes with conversion. The sense of unity that comes from family and tribal identity is the new light of spiritual illumination that electrifies our brain as though God turned on the switch. Transformation under Heaven is identity with God, an exquisite intra-psychic reality that logic and the best arguments cannot take away.

We are programmed by nature to be in awe of that which we do not understand, and that which stands as mystery in our world activates the chemistry of our brains in a manner that logical understanding never does. We are born with DNA, configured to create a brain from which our minds emerge, that lights our intra-psychic neural network in fireworks of wonder and ecstasy. Even when we trigger the process ourselves, the sensation of belonging, unity, and being loved is almost overwhelming – a wonderful gift that we frequently use to destroy rather than create.

Logic will not destroy this natural gift of God or nature, nor will politics. And it cannot be explained by words alone. Comparing the artist, musician, or great vocalist's art to their verbal explanations, we see that art excites our passion and ignites the chemistry of our brains in a manner the artist's words cannot.

Evolution is not an enemy of theism as Dawkins asserts, but is a prior order explanation for our capacity to experience mystic states. Dawkins assertion that one must accept atheism if one accepts evolution is, therefore, not logical and absurd. His position is logical only if we remain in academic isolation and refuse to accept how the brain actually creates reality and gives us mystery. He can be permitted to argue that there is no guiding hand behind evolution, but he is without such proof. The "selfish gene" is a concept, a working tool of language that helps organize a particular thought sequence, but it carries no larger truth by which to explain humankind's experiences of altered reality. He does not explain the magic of the Other that we humans have universally experienced throughout history.

71

Acknowledging the origin of common religious experiences as being products of normal brain functioning, brain functioning that is the result of biological evolution, eliminates the basis for Dawkin-type arguments. Religion is not a foolish, death-defying creation by warped minds duping ignorant people and setting each against the other in acts of death. Religious experiences are an integral part of how our minds work, and an inevitable emergent that occurs due to the structure of our brains. Labeling this natural, normal behavior, inevitable creations by normal brains, as being the root cause of human conflict misses the point. We must confront and understand why we are who we are, not rile against the wall of illusion of who we should be. Wishing it does not make it so, which is what my grandfather with his eighth grade education used to tell me. Additionally, this same capacity to experience awe and mystery brings us science.

Atheism and theism stand together as belief systems created by our rational minds, but theism enjoys the edge, it is inextricably part of the human condition because it emerges from and uses all of our inner capacity. To understand where this capacity comes from means we no longer have to fear it. We no longer have to stand in blind awe of the magicians. We no longer have to be subject to the cruel acts of its misuse. We can acknowledge this wonderful gift and use it to create a rational world, one that we direct and control; a world based upon mutual understanding and, perhaps, even love.

I am asserting that we must first acknowledge the normal functions of our brains if we are to find peace in our world. We cannot impose order any more than we can impose love by wishing it to be. We cannot eliminate the religious experience in our psyches by saying it does not exist, regardless of how one thinks we've become religious. I believe whether natural or theistic explanations ultimately lie behind first cause will eventually become known.

When we have exhausted the progress of science, we will know what God's domain is, and what ours is. But today we stand before history, looking into a future time, knowing we are all brothers and sisters built from the same DNA, from a biological history made possible through massive explosions of stars spewing trillions of tons of organic compounds into the cosmos – organics that eventually become you and me through acts of an evolving universe that lead to our own biology. God could not have designed a more awe-inspiring universe. I am humble before its reality, and content that I have been given my own capacity to be part of this miracle, a capacity that fills me with wonder and joy. Worshipping is not just for adherents of major world religions, as every true student of science knows.

MYSTICS AND PROPHETS

Mystics who are having experiences of altered reality and claiming Divine communication are judged by different standards today. We are all forced to reinterpret the Bible and other major religious works as new knowledge becomes available. We no longer have Christianity, but rather, Christianities, as we digest works like the Nag Hammadi Library, come to understand the tens of thousands of changes made by scribes in the New Testament, or discover through psychology and neural science how our brains actually operate. Knowledge lost or suppressed by organized religion creates new evaluations and fresh interpretations through discovery, and when it reaches a critical level, as it has in today's world, we enter a paradigm shift that takes us away from chanting and dancing to create and maintain mystic ASC.

A Divine Being thought to be sent to earth by God becomes a human prophet regardless of how enamored we may be of traditional dogma. The Zeus of history is the Jesus or Mohammed of today. In like fashion, acts by historical prophets that we currently explain through normal brain functions no longer have the ring of Divine intervention. Magic becomes magic once again, and the magician is just a man. Nevertheless, divinity may be expressed as an algorithm in our DNA.

Mystic experiences coming from our minds are understood from a different perspective once we know how the mind creates these experiences of altered realities. Mystic experiences may be viewed from two different perspectives. First, they express visions equivalent to "dream programming" that represent brain-centered activities normal to our species, and we come to know these visions are not divine revelations. Or, we may think visions that are equivalent to dream programs are sent by God, because this is how God communicates with humans. Following this logic, God works through the brain and mind as this is the only possible way an all-knowing entity can communicate with the limitations of our flesh and blood. The explanations are the same, but the theist is quick to point out that God is still the prime mover in the second example.

In the first example, no deity is needed to explain the visions experienced by the shaman or prophet. Whether the explanations are seen as belonging to a shaman or a prophet only depends on the extent to which the vision is accepted by large or small groups of people, but both have brains engaged in the same activity. If the crowd is large, the vision must be from God: This is Divine intervention by numbers. The effect on individuals through group persuasion, hypnosis, or suggestion, whatever you choose to call the phenomenon, is too well understood and documented for it be God's handiwork. But historically that is how God has been defined, even though this definition of Divine communication makes God a magician. The magician is seen as doing God's work when acting like a magician. Really!

In the second example, we assume that God must work through this intra-psychic mechanism in order to communicate with humans, and continue to believe that the ultimate source of our vision is Divine as we can only know God indirectly. God is assumed to be all-knowing and beyond time, space and nature, and I am not debating the issue either way. Historically, we explain select visions and altered reality experiences as coming from somewhere outside of our psyches; from the realm of the Divine. However, once major religions are established, the organized "church" takes control of which visions are acceptable, and which are to be rejected – the case of Montanism in early Christianity being a good example.

Montanus of Phrygia had two prophetesses, Maximilla and Prisca, and all three individuals reported receiving revelations directly from God. Montanism was rejected as being heretical, with agreeable visions being incorporated into the new Christian cosmology, and disagreeable visions being rejected. As Ehrman, the chair of religious studies at North Carolina at Chapel Hill, states: "The effects of Montanism we have already seen. So long as proto-orthodox Christians like Montanus and his two female companions could claim to have direct revelations from God, there were no visible constraints to prevent heretical Christians from making comparable claims." (Ehrman, 238)

In the case of Paul, his visions were accepted as belonging to mainstream Christianity because he claimed direct inspiration from Jesus. Such is the world of organized religion; content becomes the key to acceptance and the door to legitimacy. From today's perspective, this is an odd way to prove Divine contact or inspiration. How do we know if Paul was having the equivalent of a dream program or experiencing Divine contact? How do we determine which visions are "real?" Answer: It is not by church dogma, it is not through vision content compatible with the established order, and it is not by the numbers who choose to follow those having these visions. Instead, it is the behavior of the mystic or prophet that tells the tale. So, let us put Jesus to the test, but first let me make an assumption that should seem reasonable to both the theist and the atheist.

If the shaman or prophet is engaging in behavior necessary to activate his or her intra-psychic capabilities, I assume that this person is engaging in behavior that duplicates what I do when I activate, direct and control similar experiences. With this assumption, God gets credit for being all powerful and capable of communicating when God chooses to, not when human beings engage in self-activating behaviors that trigger modified inter-neuronal connections. To assume otherwise is to make God a magician, and I know of no theistic friends who would make the assumption that God has such limited abilities.

Jesus danced and spoke in tongues with the Disciples the night before he was crucified. In the Gnostic literature this is represented by a series of letters that spell nonsense, but letters that are clearly referencing verbal utterances of Jesus and the Disciples. Expressed something like (XYCPLDEF), a string of letters that spell nothing intelligible to those unfamiliar with speaking-in-tongues. For those of us familiar with speaking-in-tongues, who enjoy the process, and can activate it on demand, Jesus was dancing and speaking-in-tongues with his Disciples.

Dancing and chanting can activate the process of speaking-in-tongues, especially when one expects it to emerge. Can the reader actually believe that an omniscient being would rely on this intra-psychic mechanism to communicate sacred messages in such an unintelligible manner?

We engage in speaking-in-tongues for its effect. Brain chemistry comes into play which energizes and lifts us, sometimes to states of ecstasy. Further, does the reader believe that God finds it necessary to excite our physical bodies and lubricate our brains with our own chemistry in this manner in order to impart Divine Wisdom?

Critical evaluation of new materials related to early Christianity like the Nag Hammadi Library provides information about John the Baptist leading a religious movement that was larger and with greater influence than that of Jesus. The Baptist was reported to be in possession of the spirit of Elijah, and from this spirit possession he derived great power and charisma. Upon his death and beheading, as murky as some of the accounts are, Jesus somehow came into possession of Elijah's spirit. Thereafter, Jesus' abilities assumed greater power, and his character and ministry became more charismatic. We can appreciate the added confidence Jesus would have possessing Elijah's spirit as he had observed its effect first-hand with the Baptist. On the cross, Jesus said: "Eloi, Eloi, lama sabachthani." He called after the spirit of Elijah. Spirit possessed, spirit lost. Commonly, a different meaning is given in the New Testament's dogmatic interpretation of Jesus on the cross when He asks why God has forsaken him, not Elijah.

I do not wish to cover the extent of Jesus' experiences of altered reality. Two should be enough to make the point. Jesus was a True Believer because he both gained and lost the spirit of Elijah. Emperor Constantine made him a Divine Manifestation sent by his Father to earth when he standardized non-Gnostic Christianity at the Council of Nicea.

The Council of Nicaea in 325 CE, from which we derive the Nicene Creed, decided Jesus' divinity by one vote. If the members present, under the orchestration of Emperor Constantine, had been familiar with altered realities, does the reader believe the vote would have remained as it was, or if the emperor had selected a different group of participants from the various Christianities existing at that time? Jesus was behaving in a manner that was very human. Speaking-in-tongues is an intra-psychic phenomenon, not a communion with God.

In his lifetime, Jesus had been a shamanic prophet of notable qualities; a shaman exhibiting the abilities of one who used behavioral techniques to activate experiences of altered realities. A growing body of literature, and works by hundreds or researchers, is coming to the same conclusion. The only addition I am making to this history is to interpret Jesus' behavior using shamanic knowledge derived from experiences of altered realities; an inside-out perspective and interpretation.

Mystics or prophets who fail this test are not in direct communication with God's message. They are communicating the equivalent of dream programs originating in their own psyches. We are no longer permitted to assume visions and messages from God are all external just because philosophies and worldviews making such claims are widely accepted by large numbers of people. Cultural processes determine wide acceptance of Christianity, Buddhism, Islam, and other major world faiths. Such is the role of the anthropologist or sociologist.

Acknowledging and understanding the source of visions, a form of dream programming, gives us the ability to separate out what is coming from God and what is coming from inside our own minds. Accepting this framework of understanding permits us to recognize the equality of religious experiences spread across all kinds of different spiritual definitions, and places the shaman and major world religious figures on a comparative plane of evaluation, a plane subject to research. Can the reader suggest a prophet of any major world religion that should not be subject to this evaluation? Quickly, the answer will be: my prophet.

77

Glen A. Just

LOVE AND SPIRIT POSSESSION

Physical love, sex, has often been used in religious ceremonies as a technique to experience the Divine, a channel to Divine communication. Greeks and Egyptians using goddesses and priestesses exploited this avenue to bring initiates closer to Heaven. Jesus is documented as sleeping naked with Lazarus, while Mary Magdalene is presented by authors such as Lynn Picknett as one who was probably involved in similar behavior, a practice carried over from Egyptian and other cults. The Ten Commandments copy the Egyptian Book of the Dead almost word for word. Other Egyptian practices also influenced early Christianity, and these practices become clearer as we discover lost and suppressed works of this common history.

This murky side of Jesus' ministry has been mostly stripped from church history, but much of it is now surfacing through desert finds and careful search of ancient archives. At any rate, Jesus was very human with his practice of frequently kissing the Magdalene on the lips, along with his enjoyment of food and wine. Whether or not he and the Magdalene had a child together remains in question. (Picknett) It is unfortunate that a clearer picture of how sex played out in early Christianity is not available to us, as it would be helpful to establish this link to altered realities.

I will tie some effects of altered realities together with romantic behavior. Visiting popular gurus in India by New Age Seekers has been going on for many decades. Women often complain afterwards that they were exploited sexually while seeking uplifting religious experiences. Speaking-in-tongues can be an experience approximating orgasm, if not actually triggering one, for some. Being possessed by an evil spirit can cause the mentally ill to commit horrendous acts of sexual cruelty that, in their confused minds, shifts responsibility to an evil spirit or alter ego and away from themselves. However, the neural boxes in our brains can easily spill over into each other, and they often do in a multitude of altered realities.

When we feel love deeply it is an overwhelming feeling. Young romantics, who cannot stand to be apart, want to constantly touch, who feel they are part of each other, have a sense of, "I am you and you are me." Much Christian dogma states: "At marriage two, become one," although many have managed this exchange on their own. When I leave my body and enter a totem animal like the bear, I feel this sense of being joined, unity with the totem, merging, being one. It is a psychic act that puts us inside the other, a feeling that young lovers fully understand. Conversely, loss of a loved one, for whatever reason, leaves us with the equivalent of "Eloi, Eloi, lama sabachthani."

We know that during sexual union with intense orgasms, there is a rush of brain chemistry washing across our psyches that stops everything except the moment, and the identification is with our partner beside us, in us. Hemingway explains this effect well with Robert the main character in *For Whom the Bell Tolls*; the all encompassing moment of passion, being lifted to a higher plane, being exquisitely in another world.

For those who have many sexual partners, the feeling is temporary as the object of their love becomes the objects of their lust. Nevertheless, intra-psychic connections of altered realities can be just as intense and satisfying as they appear to involve the same brain chemistry. This intra-psychic neural crossover makes it inevitable that many people and many cultures connect Divine contact with their own sexuality.

Religious practices set forth in the Bagadavita exploit this relationship by elevating sex to a divine or near divine state. Once the practitioner of altered states of reality gains control over his physical body, all of these techniques can be easily mastered. A favorite achievement for the macho guru is to think himself into orgasm, or with a female partner, experience orgasm by sitting motionless while the two are entwined. This technique is also reported by some women as part of their religious indoctrination with the guru's love making guidance. Modified inter-neuronal connections can and do join as the transformation takes us to another world.

Glen A. Just

MYSTICS AND MORALITY

Can the True Believer who is a shaman, not just the follower who accepts the shaman's teachings, reach the highest level of morality, a level where "do unto others as you would have others do unto you" be realized? The answer must be no! Understanding what we currently know about altered realities, it is fair to ask if Jesus or Mohammed achieved a level of moral maturity found in a modern day Gandhi. Again, the answer is probably no. How can I be so sure?

Gandhi not only espoused nonviolence, he lived nonviolence. He not only espoused turning the other cheek, he actually turned the other cheek. In today's modern world we evaluate people by their behavior, and take a jaundiced view of those who say, "Do as I say, and not as I do." Gandhi's behavior reflects a level of cognitive and emotional integration compatible with the highest levels of human morality, the highest level of emotional and cognitive integration which is reflected in behavior that is expressed at a universal level, and behavior that is projected on all of humanity. He is respected and looked up to by most of the world familiar with his personal life for this behavior, a behavior which matured over his life time.

To be fair, Jesus may have reached higher levels of moral behavior had he lived to a ripe old age, but he didn't. Jesus' fondness for food and wine is very un-Gandhian. Gandhi worked hard at giving up physical sex, or at least that is what his wife reported. He did not sleep naked with other men, and to my knowledge never reported being possessed by spirits. You can do your own interpretation with Mohammed.

Other behaviors that accompany higher levels of emotional and cognitive integration are an expression of common inheritance and a sense of belonging to the whole of humanity. Gandhi clearly reached this level of behavior, and it reflects the inner peace and love we so admire in him. He didn't berate fruit bearing trees or shrubs in anger because they were without food and he was hungry. Instead, he fasted. This is a rather stark contrast between Jesus, Mohammed, and Gandhi, and one that many readers will not appreciate.

As we come to more fully understand what is going on in our psyches, and how our brains are working, our old world understanding of prophets, angels, gurus and dogmas comes under stress as many questions are raised. We are no longer permitted to hate others because our religion says we can, and sometimes even proclaim that we must. We are no longer permitted to follow the charismatic cult leader. We are no longer permitted to blow our minds with drugs in pretense that we are moving to a higher plane where contact with the spirit world occurs, or that we are activating our creativity. We become responsible citizens. We may even become nonviolent, caring, and loving individuals – world citizens.

6 - INTELLIGENT UNIVERSE

I've borrowed the title from James Gardner's *The Intelligent Universe* and will look at a few of his ideas from an intra-psychic perspective. Gardner builds his argument from an interdisciplinary model that leads to his concept of a Selfish Biocosm – a universe that is intelligently constructed by design. E. O. Wilson's *Consilience* focuses on the worldwide knowledge convergence that is taking place across disciplines. Gardner insightfully demonstrates how this process of fertilization can be used to grow new branches on the tree of knowledge. In today's world, it becomes impossible to understand religion from only one perspective, especially when that perspective is internal to a specific religion's dogma. External analysis of historical world religions is fraught with endless contradictions that sort out fairly well, when we put them under the spotlight of emerging historical documents and intra-psychic knowledge.

In *Autobiography of a Ghost,* I detail my step-by-step discovery of common altered reality experiences such as spirit possession and speaking-in-tongues. As a university student, I learned how to create and control these experiences at will. Coming to know our innate religiosity this way allowed me to explain contradictions in both world and shamanic religions. In this process of discovery, I came to experience Gardner's

Selfish Biocosm personally. Through experiential self-experiments, I explored our basic religious nature and the source of the moral law and how this nature emerges with our developmental history. Reading Gardner, I was surprised by the similarity of conclusions I drew from my experiences, which originated from childhood trauma and neglect, and those he draws from interdisciplinary analysis. I will elaborate on some of the insights that emerge from intra-psychic analysis by combining these insights with speculation and argument from Gardner.

But let me quickly point out that all of my experiential self-experiments can be replicated by researchers in psychology and the neurosciences. What I have documented from self experiments, others can recreate empirically. I am stating that the moral code that is built into our DNA is entirely subject to research, and the emergence of the moral code from our psyches directly supports Gardner's argument for an intelligent universe – the Selfish Biocosm.

Quoting Gardner's *The Intelligent Universe,* let me share some of the scaffold that supports his argument: Astronomer Sir Fred Hoyle: "A common sense interpretation of the facts suggests that a superintellect has monkeyed with physics, as well as chemistry and biology, and that there are no blind forces worth speaking about in nature." (19)

Physicist Freeman Dyson: "Here on this small planet, mind has infiltrated matter and has taken control." (22)

Galileo: "Philosophy is written in this grand book—I mean the universe—which stands continually open to our gaze. But the book cannot be understood unless one first learns to comprehend the language and read the characters in which it is written." (23)

Gardner on philosopher Mark Bedau: "Just to be clear, Bedau is not arguing that evolution produces living beings. Rather he is contending that the evolutionary process itself is the essence of life." (63)

Continuing with Bedau: "The primary forms of life are none other than the supply adapting systems themselves. Other living entities are alive by virtue of bearing an appropriate relationship to a supply adapting system; they are secondary forms of life. In other words, the structure built into nature, the algorithm is the system of life."

Gardner on Complexity theorist Stuart Kaufman: "... natural selection is aided by a hidden 'hand-maiden' – a deep seated propensity for self-organization embedded in both animate and inanimate nature." (64)

The work of Kaufman and the "think tank" at the Santa Fe Institute has helped many of us re-conceptualize evolution at a number of different levels, from biological to the natural universe. I believe what we experience moving across the landscape of external and intra-psychic realities is an intuitive sense of the hidden " hand-maiden"; a sense of moving across the universe's ocean of wave functions that transports life into the controlling role upon which our future depends. The idea of emergence in this cosmic process of evolution and subsequent expressions of this process begs understanding. Religious interpretations that deny an Intelligent Universe this level of complexity must justify themselves.

Gardner has cut a deep scratch into the interdisciplinary world of an intelligent universe, and concilience of the Wilson variety is necessary for us to talk intelligently about almost any subject in our modern world. Intra-psychic analysis, I am arguing, adds credibility to the concept of an intelligent universe by making key assumptions applicable to the human condition researchable. Further, I think Gardner's idea of the Selfish Biocosm is supported with the researchable hypothesis that the moral law is built into the substrate of nature, into the complexity of an intelligent universe, and argue further that this inherent quality is necessary to insure that life remains part of this cosmic unfolding. Life begets consciousness, and consciousness is somehow necessary to the Universe. All roads lead to Rome; knowledge from many disciplines, when it reflects a comprehensive approach to reality and consciousness, leads us to compatible conclusions.

Our gigantic cosmos has created life on Mother Earth, and most likely throughout its entire domain. It has and is creating life, if not intelligent life, by an innate order that appears to be planned. All organisms from bacteria to humans are an inevitable product of a fine tuned universe whose algorithm creates the evolutionary process driving life itself. Life creates order, and as we come to know the process intimately and approach duplicating it, the wonder of it all only increases. Order appears key to the process.

Mark Bedau states that life not only has directionality, but "robust directionality." I am arguing that this directionality and robustness is partially expressed through our innate religiosity from which we derive the moral code, and both originate in the algorithms of our DNA. Simply, life without purpose, or a super intelligent entity creating life without a moral code built in, cannot provide a guaranteed future for the universe. *Sum ergo cogito:* I am, therefore I think, not I think, therefore I am. *Ergo cogito sum* seems to express the causative direction correctly. This is evolution, not word games.

My argument throughout *Ghost* and now *Mystic* sets forth a mechanism that is within life itself. Inherent religiosity is a byproduct of the algorithm directed by a fine tuned universe which creates conscious beings like you and me; beings capable of supporting life, and the universe's continuance. Anthropocentrically to assume a God of limited ability made this possible only on one small planet, in this immense and perhaps timeless universe, seems absurd to the extreme. Different rules for life on different planets; this is not a concept of a universal God in an Intelligent Universe. The question becomes: Will world religions eventually come to accept a monotheistic vision of God?

COSMOCENTRIC UNIVERSE

Science captures our minds and lets us fly to the far corners of the universe; lets us probe the critical forces of physics which drive the universe, and takes us to the recesses of our minds – inaccessible corners of self long excluded from the consciousness of consciousness. We are transported from the small anthropocentric world of primitive shamanism and its continuance in world religions to join with an ever-expanding vision of the Intelligent Universe. Knowledge transformed, with visions electrifying! Intra-psychic reality meets cosmic universality as we step beyond the bounds of little gods into today's world where understanding is driven by consilience, and where an anthropocentric and limited God becomes infinite in *The Intelligent Universe.*

The human mind, encapsulated by mysticism, does not logically give up its religious dogmas. Intellect does not create religion and religious dogma. Deep-seated forces emerging from our algorithmic DNA create our little gods and our larger God. This is an unacceptable paradigm shift for those who remove the religious part of their minds from universal laws of nature, and thereby, separate themselves from an Intelligent Universe.

I accept Gardner's argument that: a) God becomes the Intelligent Universe through the innate qualities of biology, and, b) biology is constructed to evolve into the mind of God. c) I add that this substrate of consciousness is driven by a universal mechanism designed to express itself through the moral law, and a conscious striving for unity. The evolution of social consciousness depends on the moral law. This last assumption is not armchair philosophy, but a hypothesis subject to research, since morality and unity emerge from our innate biology, from the algorithms in our DNA. We should strive to understand this larger meaning.

My personal experience with the God syndrome as it is often viewed through the eyes of science, moves me from anthropocentrism to cosmocentrism. An anthropocentric world is the world of a Saint Augustine or Saint Aquinas, intelligent souls of history mired in the darkness of pre-scientific thought. But what of this mechanism from which the moral law emerges, the biology of God's mind, this lovely algorithm of consciousness? What does it all mean?

The evolutionary mechanism expressed in our universal religiosity is not necessary in a world created by blind chance. Why does the universe need life? Why does life need a moral law? Answer: morality is somehow central to life, and the universe's continued existence. In humankinds utopian condition, our higher levels of maturity brings us to identify with all other humans, with all life, and indeed, with the entire cosmos and every atom and energy force within it. We come to identify with all that makes life possible. Truly a strange phenomenon, if life is an accident of nature. When we add analysis of this universal mechanism to Gardner, I contend, we move one step closer to finding our souls, our place, and our purpose in an Intelligent Universe.

Cosmocentric religiosity is life made eternal as we come to join the mind of God through our understanding of this intricate edifice with its fine tuned laws, which inevitably brings forth life; life which is so designed that we can join this super-intellect in shared consciousness as we gain knowledge through the biology of life's own design. The equations of physics are amazing. Hawking points out that one part less or more in this fine tuning (ten to the tenth power) and the universe either collapses or becomes empty in a few million years. This fact is much more amazing than using chanting to direct one's disciples to speak-in-tongues. As Freeman Dyson notes: "The mind of God is the natural culmination of the mind of humans" (Gardner: 161)

Out-of-body psychic trips that took me to the beginning of time support this subjective reality, a reality consolidated around cosmic unity. Additionally, a total sense of unity emerged as I came to feel that I was part of everything in the cosmos. I came away from my Genesis Journey with an overwhelming sense that life and the universe are eternal. I cannot believe that this is somehow a unique feature of my mind. Rather, it's a feeling shared across cultures and histories, one that is universally expressed as part of our basic human nature when we permit ourselves to go there. The universe does not need to be an emerging biosphere as Gardner speculates, as mass does not equate with condition. But the mind of the universe does need this level of consciousness. And, clearly, the universe does seem to be unquestionably constructed to support life and minds with this level of consciousness.

Gardner: "… the emergence of life and the evolution of intelligence is literally pre-programmed by the laws and constants of physics, which function similar to cosmic DNA." (193) It is exciting to think that "the laws of the universe have engineered their own comprehension." (211) Gardner continues:

Glen A. Just

"The unknown super-intelligence that preceded us, Hoyle believed, put together as a 'deliberate act of creation' a universe that was suitable for carbon-based life, and the evolution of intelligence." (215)

Lee Smolin describes this scenario as you and me living in a "participatory universe," and as a cosmic shaman. I say amen. As we come to understand that religion is not a local event, an anthropocentric event, the mind of God is a mind that will be known throughout the universe. Planet Earth is just one speck, but a speck that reflects this intelligence. Steven Dick asserts that we are not the center of life, but rather, that we are a product of the larger cosmic order.

RELIGION IS SIMPLE

Religion is so simple. Why do we make it so difficult? As we emerge from the cave of religious darkness, we come to experience the light of science illuminating the blind spots of our own religious nature, and in this enlightenment we experience unity, joy, and the loving embrace of the hidden hand of God placed gently on our shoulder. And with the deeper interpretation of sociobiology, we discover the universal matrix from which human nature emerges. Twentieth Century sociology's standard model of man being born with a blank slate (tabula rasa) becomes shredded and tossed into the dustbin of history.

Dennet's assertion, with his construct of memes making religion immune to disproof, no longer has utility. Constructs that reify social imagination and attempt to explain religious phenomena as being derived from culture rather than our own psyches are doomed to join sociology's Twentieth Century's standard model. We come to understand that our religious feeling and wonder toward a God-written universe that drives the scientific mind, are one. The mind of science reflects the laws of an intelligent universe. How could it be otherwise?

I am contending that it is our religious nature, which is an extension of biology and life itself, which is an extension of the fine tuned equations of physics that is our salvation. This is contrary to Dawkins' position, as he sees religion as our ruination. Failing to understand the relationship between our religious nature and the evolutionary marvel we have been exploring is the problem, not historical religious dogmas whose contradictions are slowly disappearing under the careful eye of science. I am by nature a religious being. My religiosity is built into the algorithms of my DNA. And, whatever miniscule part of this Intelligent Universe I am privileged to share I know that it delights my soul. If God and the Intelligent Universe are one, and I can find no difference, then we are destined to be joined in Heaven, whatever Heaven might be.

A fine tuned universe is more than the equations of physics. It is physics expressed through biology directing the psychological equation that becomes our fine tuned psyche. One is dependent on the other. God's all-knowing intellect is life's beginning and final stage of evolution. Biology is fine tuned throughout the universe to recreate the moral law, for without the moral law, there is no assurance that higher life forms will continue. Without higher life forms, there is no God, if intelligent life is part of this eternal cycle.

In our cosmocentric universe we are not afraid of humankind's future. We are not afraid of biology, and machines being merged to create a greater intelligence. We are not cowed by the draconian speculations of artificial intelligence as we come to embrace unity, and a stage of future human development where the moral law is or can be expressed universally. This is the experience of the cosmic shaman: Inside-out, not outside-in.

At this point I need to say a few things about introspective knowledge of thought as discussed by neural scientists like LeDoux: "... introspective knowledge of thought processes provides a highly inaccurate window into the mind, even in mundane (non-traumatic) situations." (LeDoux, 1996, 245)

I generally agree with LeDoux and most careful researchers in this regard, however, I quickly add that respect for the average reader's ability was notably absent in the shape of Freud's ego, and much of this egoism has been continued. What has been lacking is careful research into the methodology of introspective insights that many of us can provide. To dismiss all of us outright, I believe, is a gross oversight if not outright arrogance.

Further, I am challenging psychologists, neural scientists, and developmental biologists to jointly publish their case studies rather than treating subjects as passive bacteria on a slide being examined under their favorite microscope. Providing guidelines in this process of scientific inquiry is long overdue. Lastly, failure to include subjects as feeling, thinking beings has left the mind of the mystic up to interpretation by all manner of religious charlatans.

I think that there is a contribution that individuals like me can make. My contribution is somewhat limited by the restraints of history imposed by the assumption that introspective knowledge is not reliable. It will cost science nothing to look at the matter from the inside out, and in doing so, clarify methodology. This is especially true in the 21st Century when technology permits us to watch the brain "objectively" as subjective experiences are reported.

We live in a unique period of history, being the first humans to understand our religious nature, and knowing God through the extension of the intelligent laws of science. Why would anyone prefer dogma or perpetual blindness to this option? Coming to understand that higher life forms emerge from and are integral to an Intelligent Universe's intellect, an intellect which has pre-programmed the moral law in our human form, demands that we accept responsibility for all life, for our world, and the future of our one and only known universe. We need only fear the future if we reject our own religiosity, and fail to comprehend the lessons taught by the algorithms in our DNA. Our immediate task is to create a world that permits our human nature to be fully realized and expressed.

We eliminate the historical destruction wrought by immature minds, and along with it extreme psychopathy, by understanding our religious nature and who we are. We embrace the selfish Biocosm when we understand our innate capacities. Love throughout humanity becomes a reality as we provide the conditions for every child to become fully human. This is not an impossible road to travel if we wish to reach the stars. Making this future possible for every child is our first step to realizing our full humanity.

Logic and science combine to dictate that it is time to embrace a monotheistic concept of God: The one infinite, all knowing, timeless, and loving God that emerges from an understanding of our basic human nature, a God who emerges step-by-step from the probing minds that combine science, religion and philosophy, a God whom we can assume understands Its own intellect that is free of the dogmas of historical shamans and Roman Emperors, a God who has given us the capacity to know the deepest secrets of our psyches, a God who has revealed the algorithms of life through the equations of mathematics.

A God of the Intelligent Universe who says: "Those equations are my equations." We cannot ignore the secret wonders of mathematics in an Intelligent Universe. If Gardner is correct about an Intelligent Universe, the mystery of why mathematics so closely parallels the real forces and structure of nature is no longer a mystery.

7 - GOD'S HANDMAIDEN AND DESCARTES ERROR

SCRAMBLED NEURAL NETWORKS

Altered reality experiences are like movies in our mind, and are just as real as any other experience that the mind processes. "Movies" in our mind must involve related changes in brain chemistry, as well as being able to activate any of our senses and the neural networks that connect them. All of our senses can be and are open to inter-neuronal exchanges during these experiences. Further, the mind, as it creates an altered reality, is composing a living story that can draw upon anything the brain has recorded from external experiences, as well as whatever it has created whole from a myriad of internal sensory re-combinations, either combinations remembered, or created especially for the episode. As most comprehensive beginning psychology texts demonstrate, we never experience the external world raw and in the buff. We always experience the external world in terms of our sensory processing. Alter the processing, and we alter the externally or internally constructed reality.

A simple example of our brain altering an external reality comes from our understanding of light as it enters our eyes and is passed on to the brain. The one hundred million light sensitive cells in our eyes receive external images, photons, but only one million individual connections enter the brain, a reduction of 1:100. This visual reduction process is functional and efficient; however, it also limits our mind's ability to accurately perceive what is external, as this processing always creates modifications. Additionally, the eye is sensitive to a limited range of wavelengths, and color is created in the brain itself.

We perceive a person's features outlined in dim light, but not extensive detail. We have a fairly complete sense that we can identify this person from the brain's reconstruction, which is different from the detail that actually hit the eyes surface in our act of seeing. For example, work with criminal witnesses demonstrates how inaccurate our perception is even when someone's life is on the line. Further, this visual modification does not act alone, but involves numerous other neural connections interacting across our brain that functionally serves as a central coordinating processor, the function that I have been referring to as the mind's Controller.

An interesting awareness that develops from dream programming, as I've described the process earlier, is the permanent creation of memories from the dreams themselves. When I dream program, I create characters and scenes that later appear on their own in new un-programmed dreams. They are treated in my normal dreams just as factually as events that have occurred in my real life. My sleeping mind treats self-created dream materials as being of equal value to objects in my external world.

I am not hallucinating in my sleep, as I can identify the source of this material. Further, I cannot interpret my dreams without this awareness; a process that Freud was unaware of, and one that the non-shaman informed psychologist might find confusing. Note, however, that normal dream content that is not under the dreamer's control can be treated in later dreams as factual material, just as easily as programmed content.

Identifying mind-manufactured movie material provided me with additional insight into the reality of reincarnation journeys. Once created, these scenes and episodes can and do become part of our permanent autobiographical history. They share a reality equal to one's everyday experiences. They become self-generated memories that equate the reality in our mind with our external world reality. They become fascinating "old friends" that we are reluctant to give up. (I am not referring to a psychotic episode or a hallucination.) For example, individuals who believe they are returning to former lives, and also believe they have been reincarnated, have this reality, and function normally in all other areas of life. Not only are they not bothered by these experiences, but often enjoy sharing them with others as: "In my former life, I was an Indian Chief of the Great Plains."

It helps me understand the True Believer who enters a former life and experiences it as total reality. My attention in this analysis is focused on how the brain is creating reality when it mixes intra-psychic materials with externally experienced objects. A person who does not engage in dream analysis would never know the difference between these two realities. He or she would not be able to sort out the movie in their mind and what is happening externally; both would be experienced as coming from two different worlds that are equally real. The uninformed mystic mind lives in a different reality shared by ASC and the external world reality. He or she becomes the True Believer.

Mystic or altered state experiences can use any of the brain's senses: smell, sight, taste, hearing, touch, or any combination of them in the same manner that our senses are activated in normal states of consciousness, and sometimes even cross-mix the senses. I am assuming, therefore, that the same neural networks are at play in coordinating real life experiences as they are when coordinating altered states of reality. However, at the highest level of consciousness, something else must happen. The movie in our mind takes on a reality equal to normal experiences, and the individual becomes convinced the experience has taken them to a different place, or they were actually in communication with God. For those who are having a shamanic experience but are unaware that they have created these mystic states, the experiences are treated as being real, and are attributed to something happening outside of their physical body. They see their movie as something under the control of the spirit world perhaps, or experiences set in motion by God's handiwork.

Our natural tendency to perceive intra-psychic experiences as being external must be integral to how the self is constructed in the mind. The details of this process of mind constructing self is delightful to follow, and neural scientists like Damasio and LeDoux can provide hours of delightful reading. Nevertheless, this natural tendency to externalize intra-psychic phenomena has misled much of psychology, philosophy, and religion until modern times.

For psychotics, who are not engaging a mystic ritual as the traditional shaman or priest does, the experience feels totally beyond their control. Compare this to the shaman who is aware that he has initiated the process, an awareness that I have shared with my reader and one that certain "gurus" have obviously come to know as they manipulate their followers.

Historically, individuals experiencing altered realities have been convinced that their inherited cultural interpretations must be explaining what is happening to them. They are visiting Heaven or Hell, entering the dream time of their ancestors, or speaking directly with God or God's servants. These explanations have almost always been attributed to the supernatural, as is commonly noted in historical explanations found in world religions.

This interpretation is unfortunate, because it has removed mystic states from scientific analysis, and left us ignorant of related brain functions and mind activities. Mystic interpretations of these naturally occurring mental states have contributed to our not understanding or pursuing consciousness scientifically until the last part of the 20th Century. Furthermore, it has reduced our understanding of how the self is created. It has withheld knowledge of our true religious nature, and kept untold generations from exploring phenomena of our own minds by assuming that these phenomena existed externally to our brains and bodies, and were beyond the realm of science.

Assuming that related constructs are of external or "supernatural" origin has been common to Western Philosophy, as is the case with Descartes, Kant, and others including linguists such as Chomsky. Further, this practice has continued into modern times by dominating entire university departments. It is the norm for many religious scholars. Confronting this reification process by noted academics has not been an easy task for students, and again, we can thank Damasio, neural scientists, and a broadly defined group of psychologists for helping us bring body-centered consciousness to public awareness.

Neural science and behavioral psychology are aware of related kinds of brain plasticity that produce altered perceptions, and here I use plasticity to mean newly formed or unusual neural pathways. This occurs when normal senses fail to process in typical fashion as is the case with anosognosia or asomatognosia. We have considerable research available to check the emergence of unusual or abnormal neural network configurations, although applying any of this scientific knowledge to religion has generally been studiously avoided. In *Autobiography of a Ghost,* I provide considerable detail about my own developmental history in order to document how I discovered altered realities and learned to create and control them. I am intimately aware of the historical backlash that came from many traditional psychologists, psychiatrists, and philosophers, let alone the avalanche of verbal abuse common from select religious practitioners.

DAMASIO AND THE MYSTIC MIND

When I read Damasio's *Descartes Error* shortly after it came out in 1994, I was impressed with how he handled Western Dualism and Descartes' thinking. Descartes places mind functions outside of the body in a manner common to most religious beliefs, at least traditional religious beliefs, and Damasio builds his entire story in opposition to the disembodied self. Damasio also wrestles with the state of consciousness, which is not an easy task. But he wrestles well. He also notes that attempts to study consciousness when he first entered the field were something to be avoided, and a sure way to miss tenure and solicit ridicule.

My self-struggle to explain altered reality experiences received a major boost from his analysis, and gave me additional insight into what was probably happening in my own brain and mind when I entered shamanic states. I thank him for this gift of insight, which I will share with the reader, earth bound ideas that helped me more fully understand the other world flights of my shamanic mind. But most of all, Damasio gave me hope that we were entering an era when these discussions would not only be possible at the level of respected university departments, but encouraged.

In *Descartes Error,* Damasio says: "... the body, as represented in the brain, may constitute the indispensable frame of reference for the neural processes that we experience as the mind; that our very organism rather than some absolute external reality is used as the ground reference for the construction we make of the world around us and for the construction of the ever-present sense of subjectivity that is part and parcel to our experiences; that are our most refined thoughts and best actions, our greatest joys and deepest sorrows, uses the body as a yardstick" (xvi).

He refines this explanation considerably as his story unfolds, but let me interpret what this means to a shamanic mind, a mind that is looking at intra-psychic experiences from the inside out.

I puzzled over my real-to-life experiences being out of body, and it mattered not whether I was a five year old child flying over the countryside twenty feet above solid earth, or a sixty five year old visiting the Big Bang and the beginning of time. As a child, it was beyond my comprehension to think that I was flying without my body. My body felt just as attached flying as it did playing on the ground. Damasio's thesis fully supports my "flying experiences," as my body remained my frame of reference. It is impossible for us to leave it behind and still be conscious of what we are doing. However, because we take our body with us as reference when we have shamanic experiences, we come to feel with certainty that our experiences are real, that we do enter another reality, or another world.

However, let me compare my death experience at two years of age with asomatognosia, and Damasio's patient, LB. In *The Feeling of What Happens* he states: "The patient had a small stroke involving a select part of the right somatosensory cortices." He further notes that in some of the seizure episodes resulting from scarred brain tissue "… the patient reported being unable to feel her body…" (214). When I died in the hospital as a small child, I distinctly felt I was leaving my body, (I didn't feel my body) and started my journey to Heaven and met the angels. I distinctly remember rejecting their invitation to Heaven and returned to my body. A strange feeling when I compare it to what I am experiencing writing these words in a normal state of consciousness. My ASC resulted from smothering and brain damage and approximated an asomatognosia experience.

Let me make another comparison with "locked-in" syndrome where the affected person is conscious of everything taking place around him but cannot move any part of his body except for moving the eyes up and down like he is performing keystrokes on a computer. This person can hear speaking and understand words, but cannot speak or move. I am guessing that my hospitalization approximated this condition, because the doctor pronounced me dead and covered me with a sheet. If my father had not lingered talking with the doctor and nurse, I could easily have been sent off to the morgue.

I was two years old, but I had experienced death and sickness in our family with Uncle Gus, who died of a brain tumor. My generation lived with birth, sickness, and death in our homes, and it was accompanied by history's cultural interpretations. I can imagine that when the doctor pronounced me dead and my body's neuronal connection to consciousness ceased, the awareness of my little mind naturally went off to Heaven. All the images accompanying this out-of-body experience were constructed from my tiny and limited world of experience.

I know my conscious mind was put into a coma-like state by Mother's smothering attack, and as my consciousness began to return in the hospital, I would have started to process the conversations taking place around me. I will never know the unique pattern of brain damage that I suffered, but it evidenced symptoms similar to those discussed above. My early ability to use speech was lost, I learned to walk again as this function was also lost, and I suffered episodes of epileptic fits as described later by mother. Movement pathways to the brain had been destroyed or partially shut down, but my consciousness remained intact as I returned to life in the hospital. What endless ways we have to construct mystic minds, but all of these constructions build on the architecture of our neural capacities.

In *The Feeling of What Happens,* Damasio states: "Impaired extended consciousness possibly contributes to the dissolution of self associated with states of depersonalization and with states of mystical selflessness, and the same is true of the controversial condition of multiple personalities." Continuing, he notes that with impaired extended consciousness, "The sense of wakefulness is present; so is the sense that images are being made and attended; and so is the sense of being alive and capable of feeling." (216) This analysis of impaired extended consciousness fits perfectly with my experience of dying as a toddler; "mystical selflessness," as he refers to this state, is depersonalized as one has a sense of looking at another you that is you, while still being conscious in the primary self.

One more reflection on the cognitive state of my near death experience: As the angels turned from being sparkling distant lights into human figures, I was bathed in a sense of well being and love, a feeling state that is often reported by others with death experiences like mine. The locked-in syndrome, and Damasio reports a case example in *The Feeling of What Happens,* produces a state of inner calm, peace, and well being. (243) He describes this state as a positive gift given to those who suffer such a cruel condition. My speculation is retrospective over many years, but the memories remain strong even if they may have become modified with time. To further quote Damasio: "Knowledge will help being." (316)

Additionally, Damasio goes on to say that, "The mental representation of the autobiographical self is so impoverished that the mind does not know where this self comes from or where it is headed." (216-217) I might add that at two years of age my autobiographical self had a long way to go before it knew where it was headed. But then, as a two year old, I was headed for Heaven accompanied by angels.

Glen A. Just

Interpreting my death scenario, using Damasio, helps me bring this experience into the neural scientist's model and continues to support basic contentions made in *Autobiography of a Ghost* and now, this work. Retrospectively, I know as a child that my understanding of self, others, and the universe was very limited. I accepted the views of those around me without question. I am quite sure that discussions in the hospital of my dying and going to Heaven provided the interpretive framework for this culturally defined reality. Additionally, I earlier recounted my Uncle Gus dying of a brain tumor and having an adult dream where he sits under a tree in our yard where fall leaves are blowing past him. Suddenly he begins to erode, and blows away with the wind. Dust to dust – and Heaven bound.

I can see the preacher standing over the cemetery's grave. I can see the angels reaching for me as they prepare to take me to Heaven, as I experience their warmth and love, as my disembodied mind floats effortlessly in a Zen trance much like my later practice of Zen driving. Knowledge does come together in the modern world, and these are exciting times. "Blind" introspection does not capture our minds; it is for the blind, but I can choose to see, as others may.

Out-of-body experiences must be scrambling neural circuits in a similar fashion to asomatognosia or locked-in syndrome. I was not tested for brain damage as a toddler, but I did lose my early speech and walking abilities, thereby indicating some type of brain damage. As a child and adolescent when I watched the Northern Lights or a tumultuous thunder storm, I would feel transported into the lights or the storm and merge with the pulsing energy; the energy of my mind mingling, playing and being totally free. I believe my childhood trauma left me with a permanent capacity to reengage the operative neural functions created by my Mother's acts of smothering, and the reconfigured neural pattern left open after my recovery.

Permit me as an aside to offer a few thoughts on experiential self-experiments of the type I have practiced life-long. Initially, I simply had an out-of-body experience happen to me as a toddler. But I quickly learned to enjoy flying and being" being out-of-body, and by the time I recovered from my death experience and related loss of speech and walking functions, I was "flying" regularly. I discovered Einstein's "gedanken" or thought experiments when I read his work on relativity and special relativity after being hospitalized with pneumonia when I was fifteen. Thought experiments seemed just as natural to me as flying, and both offered diversion and fun for an isolated country boy seeking the companionship of words.

Thought experiments were the answer to a country boy's dreams. There was no equipment, no money needed, and the experiments could be performed while riding on a tractor cultivating, or watching the constellations on a warm summer's evening. Once I discovered developmental psychology and Skinnerian behavior modification at the university, self-experiments became an on-going part of my life. Is "gedanken" subjective and introspective, or can it be objective? Poor Einstein!

It is this unique history, one that I frequently had to struggle with, that brought me to question the traditional Freudian models of dreams and the self: Kantian logic and Chomskyan linguistics. Traditional religion took its place in the wastebasket along with Descartes, Kant and other mystics, except that the world did not consider these "others" as mystics. The world, when it is confronted with a new paradigm, does not stop revolving easily, to paraphrase Coelhoe in *The Alchemist.*

Going back to Damasio in *Descartes Error:* "Feelings are just as cognitive as other percepts." (xv) "Feelings form the base for what humans have described for millennia as the human soul or spirit." (xvi) Ah, such magical words, and such a comforting explanation for one who spent years trying to identify the sources of his own soul, a soul that often flew around the countryside and universe.

Out-of-body experiences create a problem for those observing our behavior while we are busy having them. The body doesn't move, but we are still experiencing reincarnation, spirit possession, astral flight, or some other mystic state. There must be something immaterial that resides in us; something that can come and go. It is called the soul, as Damasio says.

Once we accept that feelings are an integral part of our consciousness, and Damasio makes it very difficult to ignore them, we come to realize that consciousness is maintained by

Glen A. Just

both the neural and chemical feedback from our body to key centers throughout our brain. With these insights, I can more fully account for my unusual experiences as a shaman.

The nice thing about Damasio's hypotheses is that they are testable, as I believe other aspects of altered realities are testable (see Epilogue). Once Descartes error is cornered, once Kantian mysticism is dispensed with, once religious dogma that keeps us from understanding our religious nature is overcome, we are free to explore answers according to the rules of science, as we do with every other area of human inquiry. I firmly believe that we must pursue the neural scientist's path to enlightenment if we are to permanently bridge the gap between science and religion. The enlightenment comes not through prayer, although prayer's positive aspects are well documented in the placebo effect, but through an understanding of our most basic human capacities. Thanks, Antonio!

Paraphrasing Damasio: Mind embodied brain; mind embodied body... separation is fictional (Descartes Error, 118). We can no longer attempt to explain religion without neural science. We cannot explain consciousness without neural science. We cannot understand altered states of reality without neural science. And we can no longer pretend that projections from our minds represent external realities. As early Christian Gnostics believed: God is within us, and God is to be experienced, not externalized.

We know that duplicating muscle movements creates feelings that are normally expressed by those movements. Actors who do not learn to separate the two feel drained after performances, while actors who can separate the two do not feel drained emotionally, although they may be physically tired. However, performances experienced as a shaman do not leave me feeling drained. Just the opposite; I feel lifted, inspired, energized, and alive. For example, speaking-in-tongues produces a chemical high when all those neural transmitters kick in.

My friend, who enjoys automatic writing, can write for hours without tiring her arm; a practice I always found intriguing as she is not very athletic. I do not know why muscles never seem to tire under altered states, however, it would be interesting to

102

test muscle fatigue using modern technology to determine what is happening. Do our muscles tire and we just do not notice the effect as our brain chooses to ignore its own messages? I am guessing, but adrenaline output somehow gets modified during these altered reality adventures and stays under control.

Using autosuggestion to stay alert while driving, or simply speaking-in-tongues does not give me the same sense of fatigue as long distance driving without hypnosis. I doubt that muscles are capable of expressing themselves differently when the mind is in an altered state, however, I am positive that my mind shuts out fatigue and keeps feeding energy to the action itself. If I undergo an intense period of concentration, such as cramming for exams over an eight hour period of time, as I did as a university undergraduate, I also experience very little fatigue or loss of concentration, even though these marathons were usually accompanied by two to four hours of sleep, cramming being what it is.

Using meditation in a similar psychic state one can perform muscle feats that are not normally possible, for example, keeping one's arm fully extended for an hour. I am speculating that this neural modification mechanism is operating when religious zealots go into battle and perform amazing feats.

Another fun area for the neural scientists to explore is our lack of fatigue during altered states, not going into battle, but how the mind is tricked not to experience fatigue when our neural channels are changed this way. Our altered consciousness seems to have greater focus and energy supply at these times than when we are in our normal state of consciousness. Brain regulatory mechanisms in altered states do not overreact, but just supply us with appropriate, ongoing amounts of adrenaline over extended periods of time. This seems to eliminate fatigue associated with normal marathon activities.

Damasio on evolution: "… the mind exists in and for an integrated organism: our minds would not be the way they are if it were not for the interplay of body and brain during evolution, during individual development, and at the current moment." (*Descartes Error,* xvi) Indirectly, I believe Damasio is supporting my thesis for an algorithm being built into our DNA, one that helps a conscience guided by moral law to emerge, a conscience that has rid itself of conflicting inputs and fragmented throughputs when we are adequately nurtured and supported.

Intra-psychically during altered states, we feel an intense sense of unity. I believe this sense of unity is experienced to a higher degree during altered reality states for two reasons: First, we are blocking out unrelated inputs from our environment, and secondly, it is necessary to create a strengthened feedback loop in the neural network in order to have the experience. There is a special kind of calm that floods across our neural pathways during these moments; one that many individuals in religious orders search for through meditation or quiet contemplation.

Damasio says: "The organism interacts with the environment as an ensemble: the interaction is neither of the body alone nor of the brain alone…The physical operations that we call mind are derived from the structural and functional ensemble rather than from the brain alone: mental phenomena can be fully understood only in the context of an organism interacting in an environment." *(Descartes Error,* xvi) Additionally, Damasio states about background feelings that "… without them, the very core of your representation of self would be broken," (151) and, "… background body sense is continuous, although one may hardly notice it." (152)

I believe this model of the human organism helps explain the perceived reality of the religious mystic. And if the reader accepts my argument that human beings are religious by nature, and that this innate nature emerges from our DNA, then the body-mind ensemble helps us explain why we feel and act the way we do. We can no more rid ourselves of our religious nature than we can be conscious and disconnect from the mind-body ensemble as Damasio presents it.

Additionally, the mind-body ensemble makes it inevitable that our projections of self (soul) are experienced as occurring along with our physical bodies. Further, this internal reality leads some of us to believe that our physical bodies enter the other world, Heaven, with our soul. The background of "core self" as Damasio presents it appears as a shadow in our external flights of self.

BRAIN DAMAGE

Smothering by Mother that led to my hospitalization as a toddler must have damaged a number of brain centers, as early speech and walking abilities were lost and had to be regained after I returned home. Further, I recall some episodes as late as eight years of age where I lost consciousness and would momentarily fall to the ground, but by eight the episodes were limited, and I would regain control within seconds. I don't have good recall about earlier "fainting" episodes when I first returned from the hospital, however, my mother described them as epileptic fits.

Language impairment probably reflects damage to my left temporal lobe, frontal lobe damage affecting movement, my lost ability to walk, and defects in memory and attention that followed me into university life probably occurred at the same time. Most of my life, I have experienced slight dyslexia with both letters and numbers, but mostly numbers. I loved math as a student and usually found math problems easy to master, however, when under intense pressure at the university, I would commit stupid errors transposing numbers and experienced major problems with what had been one of my favorite subjects.

I am speculating that related brain damage from Mother's smothering somehow scrambled, or rewired, parts of my brain's neural network, and this rewiring created the cosmic shaman. Damasio talks about diseases of the brain as being neurological tragedies, while character flaws – diseases of the mind – are conditions for which the individual should be shunned or punished. A major source of character disorder, I strongly feel, is socially induced but physiologically real. And psychopathy stems from parental abuse of the kind common to my family.

Neural science offers insights as neglect and abuse directly impact the brain structures in the limbic system. Physical, emotional and social support permits the individual to realize their full genetic potential. Conversely, physical structures of the brain, especially those in the limbic system, are underdeveloped with neglect and abuse as LeDoux also notes in *The Emotional Brain* (Chapter 8, 1996).

This phenomenon is now fairly well understood, and has been researched for over two decades in the United States and Europe. The exception being personnel in government and the American correctional system who fail to pay attention or for politically correct reasons will only support a system of punishment, and thereby insist that the one-legged racer must be punished for his or her inability to run the normal social race.

Damasio: "I believe also that in numerous instances the brain learns to concoct the fainter image of an 'emotional' body state without having to reenact it in the body proper." (Descartes Error, 155) I am arguing that the brain can go one step beyond a "fainter image of an 'emotional' body state..." In altered realities, as I look at these realities from the inside out as a shaman, I believe the brain can concoct an "emotional" body state that is not faint, but fully expressed, and in similar fashion, does so for those experiencing psychotic episodes.

I also believe that neural scientists will come to more fully understand consciousness and self when altered states of reality are fully explored. Speculation by Artificial Intelligence researchers as to when human intelligence can be surpassed, I suggest, must take the shaman's capacity for altered reality into consideration as well. Human capacity requires interaction between twenty billion neurons, a trillion neural connections and all their altered states as affected by brain and body chemicals. I have yet to find attempts to discuss altered realities by AI researchers, even though an improved understanding of consciousness necessitates review of this capacity, and involves the same mechanisms.

Current body input to the brain is diminished or repressed by a mind stressed by anxiety and depression, hence, the mind does vary psychically as related body state inputs change. This includes chemical as well as other inputs through neuronal exchanges taking place in the brain; therefore, emotion is induced by both neural and chemical routes.

I have previously given specific examples of how my brain repressed my body image to psychically shrink me to half size. As children, we learn to go somewhere else when impacted by extreme stress or when hyper-vigilance becomes too exhausting. We dream in school, express body tension by drumming on our desks, take flight of fancy through the school window, or if we possess shamanic capacity, we fly.

Reason and emotion intersect, according to Damasio, in the ventromedial prefrontal cortices. They also intersect in the amygdala and related limbic areas. Neurotransmitters such as dopamine and norepinephrine are sourced here. Serotonin functions to reduce aggression, thereby supporting positive social behavior. Psychologists like Doctor Kenneth Dennis from Rochester, Minnesota, are finding brain damage in over half of the serious juveniles offenders that they test. (Doctor Dennis previously conducted tests for one of the juvenile correctional treatment programs that I developed and administered.) As we become familiar with the aggression expressed by these young people, we know that it is counter-productively contained by America's current punishment model. Aggression supported by brain damage is not dealt with effectively in a system of punishment. The opposite occurs, and increased aggression results.

In my personal history, learning to control anxiety and depression, overcoming the syndrome of hyper-vigilance that I learned in childhood, and extending my ability to concentrate from twenty minutes to eight hours, permitted me to gain control over pain, vascular dilation, and heart rate, and develop other related self-controls. It also unquestionably altered my brain chemical levels. I gained control over a violent temper, anxiety, depression, and by the time I graduated with my bachelor's degree, returned three critical areas of my MMPI profile back to normal. So Damasio's discussion of how reason and emotion intersect squares completely with my own experience. Additionally, his model calls attention to interlocking similarities between altered states of reality, mental illness, and behavioral dysfunctions that put young people in lock-up.

Glen A. Just

ARROW OF TIME

More by Damasio from *Descartes Error:* "Complex organisms such as ours do more than just interact ... they also generate internal responses which constitute images (visual, auditory, somatosensory, and so on), which I postulated as the basis for mind." (90) "... mind means that an organism forms neural representations which can become images, be manipulated in a process called thought, and eventually, influence behavior by helping predict the future, plan accordingly, and choose the next action." (88-89)

These images may be generated entirely within the organism, thereby shaping and directing the mind in ways totally disconnected from the external world. This is the world of the ascetic, the monk, the recluse, the priest, the nun, or the dedicated guru. Tragic, joyful, wonderful, a loss to humanity, beautiful or disgusting – how does the reader chose to interpret the consequences? Let us agree that understanding comes before choice, and choice means that we have freedom to realize our full potential and not be slaves to dogma, or the seduction of our own minds. The wonder of knowing exceeds the joy of ritual.

There is no integrated brain site. Integration is by time, not by a theater of the mind, says Damasio. What he states provides an explanation for the Arrow of Time we humans experience, and not a small explanation at that. Without the Arrow of Time, we have no consciousness. It seems self-evident as Damasio notes that we humans never live in the present, as every moment of consciousness is built on input from our bodies, senses, and the external environment; something that has already taken place. Hence, all of our assumptions and experiences of reality are built around a process that is programmed into our psyches, our DNA. It is functional and necessary for our survival, and it may be misleading when placed in the context of altered states.

Damasio in *Descartes Error:* "...the brain is not likely to predict how all the commands... will play out in the body..." (158).

I know from an internal perspective that it cannot be any other way. When I experienced being a 6'2" giant, the shift in physical size that doubled my psychic self happened instantly, and it was shocking. But clearly, Damasio's assumption speaks directly to experiences like mine. Further, what makes the dream program real, or a hallucination for the psychotic, is surprise to the individual's mind as the controlling, the coordinating centers, for neural feedback in the brain feel overwhelmed by what is happening in the body as neuronal activity is expressed through the feedback loop to the brain, and the mind confirms this reality of neuronal input. I become the bear, fly to Heaven, talk to angels, and may become a True Believer.

Psychological tests like the MMPI do not distinguish between psychotic states and altered reality states, and I suggest that this is a major oversight. We who activate altered reality states are aware of our self-control. These mystic states do not have the same effect on our minds as psychotic states have for individuals who feel lack of control. We know we are not actively hallucinating. Even if the shaman is a True Believer, altered reality states become scenes viewed by the activating observer when he or she learns to create and direct them. Consequently, they do not arouse fear or panic, but often create awe or mystery. Clarity of understanding between these differences has been lacking in the mental health community.

Damasio: "... I see a need to posit at least two major components in the neural mechanism underlying feelings. (*Descartes Error*, 161) Spurious causal association leads to a superstitious interpretation of something that has happened to us; when the spurious alignment of emotion is with fear and the object is pervasive, phobic behavior will result." (162)

I previously discussed mind controlling cracks where I was obsessively forced to step over sidewalk cracks in the little town of Island City. Looking back, I was extremely unhappy living on the edge of town without friends, being ostracized by town kids and called names, having to fight groups of boys who thought a hick in bib overalls was an easy target, losing my dog in a traffic accident, and coming to feel totally alienated. Phobic

109

responses of this kind still loom large in my memory, and recall makes it impossible not to touch the pain of days gone by.

I could write a hundred pages of new awareness stemming from Damasio's insightful books and related research, but I will refrain. I have used him extensively as my formal training is not in neural science, and his was the first model of consciousness and how the self emerges that resonated with my shamanic history. However, the convergence of scientific knowledge across disciplines makes it impossible not to take the findings of similar study areas into consideration.

My objective in the above analysis has been to demonstrate how current research in neural science helps explain altered realities, thereby helping to further remove some of the mysticism that has surrounded religion. I am also asking the reader to take a closer look at their favorite dogmas, and give consideration to their own religious nature, as this nature naturally emerges from an expanded awareness.

I may have missed a point here and there, but I do believe the road I have been traveling, the insights I have been sharing with you, are representative of the general direction we must go if we wish to reconcile religion and science. The test, always the confirmation or rejection, comes when the rubber hits the road and we confirm or reject our hypotheses. It would be a wonderful change of paradigm if many of the traditionally religious were willing to include human nature, as revealed by science, in their understanding of our relationship to the God within each one of us. Simply, we will not know God if we do not know ourselves, and we cannot begin to understand the Intelligent Universe if we do not understand ourselves. Dogmas, sacred or secular, must give way to open minds.

8 - EMBODIED PHILOSOPHY

THE CREATOR SPEAKS

As a Cosmic Shaman, I have been looking at the intra-psychic world of consciousness and self, and have offered an interpretation from the perspective of these altered realities; realities that I created and explored subjectively. Further, I have previously compared my altered realities to contemporary and historical mystics. In my experiential explorations of the major mystic experiences supporting religions both large and small, I have found direction and enlightenment from a number of sources in psychology, neural science, philosophy, physics, world religions, and considerable experiential exploration of my own religious nature. My focus has been to bring various scientific fields together and share this interdisciplinary perspective, thereby offering further insight into what is happening in the Mystic's mind.

Seminal thinkers in the neural sciences, especially Antonio Damasio and Joseph LeDoux, have helped me gain additional insight into my own intra-psychic experiences, and what goes on in my brain and mind during these experiences. *Descartes Error,* where Damasio introduces the reader to neural science's understanding of consciousness and self, and his elaborations on feelings and emotions in *The Feeling of What Happens* and

Looking for Spinoza, have added depth to my understanding of these phenomena.

In Chapter Seven I covered some of the basic contributions of neural science that have helped further clarify our religious nature, which grounds intra-psychic experiences in body and brain. In total, streams of thought from interdisciplinary studies have helped me clarify how our religious nature brings us to create both tribal and world religions. The brain-body grounded mind clarifies experiences of altered reality in a manner that traditional religion and philosophy, which are disembodied, cannot.

One of the most helpful insights offered by Damasio is how we construct a sense of the self in the "Now." As he points out: "I am writing these words on my keyboard, and at the same time, I am aware that I am sitting at my computer, hands on keyboard, and composing these thoughts. However, "Now" for me is something that has already happened. "Now" is a split second in my past; very specifically, I am aware subjectively of living in the present, but neural processing takes a split second and leaves my functioning self in the past; my subjective "Now" always lags behind real time. Not a minor point at all in creating the reality of the "Now," a reality of consciousness and ASC."

Damasio's insight helps explain why intra-psychic altered reality seems just as real as experiences that are happening external to my self and body. Neural processing is always delayed a split second from our present, (Now) and either of the two experiences, normal or altered reality, are processed by the brain using the same scaffolding. A simple but profound insight as to why Mystics are so insistent that their experiences are real! The brain does not differentiate intra-psychic time from extra-psychic time in terms of the self's subjective reality, and the two share the same time frame and time lag in our minds. Brain functioning and neural processing dictate that the two experiences are of equal value. They are both equally real, and occur in what the brain experiences as the Now.

Lakoff and Johnson brought me to the connection between the embodied self and embodied thought in *Philosophy in the Flesh,* thereby clarifying how Western Philosophy has historically disembodied thought and helped religion perpetuate the idea that mystic experiences are occurring externally to our self and minds. Historically, if thought is disembodied, then a number of assumptions must follow.

1) The Self as Soul is separate from our bodies and brains and exists independently. Following this disembodied logic, the problem becomes: What is the Soul, and where does it come from? The answers have been convoluted and creative by people of different cultures historically.

2) If thought is separate from the mind and body as Western philosophers like Descartes and Kant have claimed, and linguists like Chomsky have proposed, then an entire edifice of thought exists separately from humankind, and we must find and explain this edifice by searching outside ourselves. A mind game that never ends, a mind game brought forward from the earliest written documents of our species, a mind game that is two legged, meaning that religion and philosophy as disembodied disciplines have supported each other, and the past continues to walk in the present.

Neural Philosophy presented by Lakoff and Johnson demonstrates that science can be brought to bear on the fundamental questions asked historically, such as What is consciousness? What is thought? What is essence? and so on. Once the edifice of mystical philosophy is unveiled, one can no longer claim superiority of method using well reasoned and seemingly logical schemes, such as Kant's "Pure Reason."

Externalizing thought, making it something that exists separately from brain and body, can no longer be supported. We come to realize that disembodied religion's days are equally limited. In E. O. Wilson's use of *Consilience*, the convergence of scientific thinking from many disciplines, which now includes philosophy, leaves religion on a lonely island in a sea of rapidly rising empirical water. The headwinds are growing too strong for the fragile structure of dogma to stand.

Lakoff and Johnson explain how the brain constructs concepts by which thought becomes reason. For example, time has two metaphors in the mind: we are passing through time, or time is passing us by. In either case, it is a metaphor of movement relative to us, the organism. As organisms, we are aware of our physical presence and movement in space, and use these constructs, these metaphors, to explain change over time.

Another metaphor is body as container: I have an inside and an outside like a container, and I use this concept to differentiate what is inside and outside of my skin. Dozens of different metaphors are presented and explained by Lakoff and Johnson, and I will not repeat them here. Readers who are unfamiliar with works such as *Philosophy in the Flesh* can spend a couple of delightful weekends digesting this material. Embodied philosophy provides a thought stream that intersects with numerous other empirical sciences such as neural science, developmental psychology, and neural linguistics.

To the Cosmic Shaman, what is significant about embodied philosophy is its grounding in empirical research, its resonance with neural science, and the ongoing discoveries in laboratories such as Damasio's. Also, its compatibility with developmental psychology, and the relationship of all of these different fields of study to the basic questions of our self and consciousness, and of our universe's beginning and evolution.

We truly live in exciting times. These are times when our religious nature can be and is being probed by science for the first time, a time when we can come to know who we really are as a religious species, a time when Cosmic Intelligence can be explored free of mysticisms, and a time when our basic nature can be understood from the standpoint of freeing ourselves from destructive dogmas that have promoted hate and mutual destruction. We discover that the Age of Enlightenment – wasn't.

I have been arguing in both *Autobiography of a Ghost* and now in *Mystic* that we cannot understand our religious nature without science, and conversely, we cannot understand religion if we remain blind to our religious nature. Further, this blindness keeps us from understanding an Intelligent Universe (God), our own religious self, and in this blindness, we perpetuate much of what has been destructive to our species and our world. Embodied self as explained by neural science, embodied philosophy in the New Era of Philosophy, and, I believe, the New Era of Embodied Religion. All come together in a modern paradigm that is finally revealing formerly hidden aspects of who we are as a species, as well as our true religious nature.

In the *Intelligent Universe*, Gardner reviews the unlikely occurrence of a cosmos like ours happening by chance, and offers a reasoned view from a scientific framework that a master intelligence is at work. His reasoned argument is based on science, and offers insight into how contemporary research in physics, astrophysics, artificial intelligence, and other interdisciplinary studies lead us to a universe that is intelligent. It is exciting speculation, and well-reasoned speculation, that finally brings us to a potentially monotheistic explanation of God. I believe that embodied religion, coming to understand our basic religious nature, moves you and me one step closer to understanding who we are and where we have been, and points out our natural place in the cosmos.

I am suggesting that our understanding of the embodied self and mind, along with an embodied philosophy, adds further support to Gardner's ideas. Lastly, the embodied Cosmic Shaman's experiences are explained when viewed from the perspectives of the neural sciences and neural philosophy. Explaining embodied altered states of reality and mysticism places all religions on equal footing regardless of whether they are long or short in historical duration, have few converts or millions, have a well thought out dogma, or are riddled with contradictions. We can no longer discuss our religious nature without empirical science at the core of this discussion.

PHILOSOPHY IN PERSON

Embodied philosophy has a number of insights that can be added to a natural explanation of our religious nature, thereby bringing us closer to understanding of how this nature naturally emerges, and how religion is an inevitable emergent of human culture. Philosophy is the second great invention of humankind's inquiring minds, and grows naturally out of our biological nature and experiences. Removing disembodied philosophy as a major leg which supports all disembodied reason, exposes religious dogmas and schemes as intriguing human thought experiments. As embodied philosophy gains increasing empirical support, it becomes impossible to argue that thought, reason, mind, and soul are entities separate from our evolutionary self and bodies. If we are to remain true to our religious nature, we will have to rethink the entire edifice that currently supports world religions. A quick look at embodied philosophy should help further clarify this assumption.

According to Lakoff and Johnson, the Cognitive Unconscious is responsible for mental images, visual and auditory images, memory and attention, grammar, emotions, conception of motor operations, etc. Ninety-five percent of thought is unconscious, but we have not traditionally known or believed this. Hence, extra-body experiences have been assumed to be real and related to the supernatural, rather than being part of that ninety-five percent of mental activity that continuously operates below our conscious level of awareness.

The supernatural, as it turns out, is inside us, embedded in all that goes on unbeknownst to the individual as the Cognitive Unconscious continues to process at a level below our conscious awareness. Combined with neural science, which explains how the individual's "Now" is always in the past, we begin to understand why altered reality experiences seem totally real. Our brains cannot function otherwise, and our minds are dependent on our brain functions. Our present moment, the moment of the "Now" if you will, is subjective, and represents experiences that have already occurred.

Lakoff and Johnson state that "Metaphysics in philosophy is, of course, supposed to characterize what is real – literally real. The irony is that such a conception of the real depends upon unconscious metaphors." (14) In other words, the constructs, metaphors that form thought, operate at a level below our awareness. Religion, like philosophy, could claim disembodied thought and spirits in the past as contemporary knowledge in neural science and neural philosophy was lacking. "Universal Laws" were created in our minds, but attributed to external sources by religion and philosophy, and then interpreted as coming from the mind of God. Once thought is placed outside our organism, it can be interpreted in endless ways and assumed to be originating from any supernatural source we envision. Historical analysis of spirits, gods, and the supernatural offers a rich variety of assumed sources. There is no end to these creative inventions, unless the religious edifice becomes strong enough to impose limitations, as Christianity did during its dark ages.

Cognitive science and neural philosophy require us to create a new, empirically responsible philosophy, and require us to apply this knowledge to a fuller understanding of our own minds as we come to know how our minds are formed, and how they function. For the theist, God cannot exist in false reasoning or false consciousness. If you are a theist, God determines Its own reality.

We do not establish reality through the inventions of our mind, and God's reality is not explained by a primitive interpretation of nature or humankind. If you are a theist, you agree that God has created us, and we are not a product of chance. If you are an atheist, natural laws are operating in biology to create the mind and consciousness, as we are coming to understand them. In either case, we have no conflict understanding how it all works; we only have differences in the assumed initial cause.

To paraphrase Einstein, God does not play tricks with his laws. Laws discovered by science appear to be even more precise than the current equations of physics. The human mind is capable of perceiving our world and the universe's beauty, and it is capable of perceiving color through our special form of consciousness and perception. It is capable of these endeavors because the Cognitive Unconscious makes color possible. The mind gives us color, where nature does not. We perceive a narrow range of electromagnetic radiation from our universe in terms of our perception, and the mind converts this radiation to color. Color exists in our subjective neural processing, and not outside of our minds in nature. Color and the multitude of historical gods are two of our wonderful creations, and they both emerge from the unique structure of our brains.

As Lakoff and Johnson state: "One of the important discoveries of cognitive science is that the conceptual systems used in the world's languages make use of a relatively small number of basic image schemes…"(35). The metaphorical content, the building blocks from which we create all our reality, are found across our species worldwide; hence, there should be little wonder at the similarity of what is created in the minds of "Homo religiosus." How could it be otherwise? Our minds construct reality from the same basic building blocks, the same basic metaphors. Our minds create the same variety of altered realities and mystic experiences, thereby leaving us with the sense that something universal must be out there rather than in here. In here, of course, being our minds and the brains that sustain them.

Lakoff and Johnson continue to explain complex metaphor as not being "…arbitrary but represent(ing) images from one's culture…" such as love is a journey metaphor, one can be stuck in a relationship metaphor, or we are spinning our wheels in this relationship metaphor. Once we mature past simple metaphors and enter the rich combinations that emerge with our physical and mental development and within our cultures, the images we create can be and are extensive.

We build our world accordingly. The traditional Eskimo culture, for example, has numerous expressions for many more types of snow than was common when I was a child in Wisconsin. I saw dry snow and wet snow, large flakes and small flakes, but I didn't see snow as the traditional Eskimo saw it. I lived in a "southern" reality, not on a piece of geography closer to the North Pole. And so it is across the world and across cultures. What we perceive and interpret depends upon place and time. We have the capacity to see our world in detail, with all its beauty and with a sense of wonder, or we can see it rough hewn.

The template from which we build basic metaphors is universal to our species, and how we construct complex metaphors is dependent upon our culture. Nevertheless, this universal capacity is activated in similar ways as when we come to be possessed by spirits, possess the spirits of other people or animals, fly out-of-body in astral travel, or journey to former lives in reincarnation. How can it be otherwise? The mind emerges from a brain built from the same neural structures, driven by the same chemistry, creating mental structures from the same building blocks, and creating altered realities that only differ by cultural content as we form complex metaphors within our own living environments.

Most of what is happening in our brains and minds is going on without our awareness, and this understanding is now without question. But within this bubbling caldron of neurons firing millions of times each second of our lives resides a locus of consciousness, the Subject (Us), according to Lakoff and Johnson. Our Subject processes our subjective experiences, directs our reason, will, and essence. (268) We feel it, and it is inseparable from our total being.

Whenever we conceptualize our inner life, there is always a subject that is the locus of reason, and we experience it as having an existence independent of our body. Further, we experience our subject as a person. It is natural, therefore, that the idea of a little person in our brains, a homunculus, should be so widespread. This subjective experience is worldwide. We all grow up with this view of our inner lives, and this view is mostly unconscious. It is quite easy for the shaman to convince the children of the world that this entity can take flight, or that it should be your master.

Lakoff and Johnson continue by acknowledging that each of us also has a Self which is responsible for everything beyond the responsibilities of our Subject, that is, our bodies, social roles, actions, histories, etc. As individuals, "… we do not have one single, unified notion of our lives." (268) As our philosophers note, we can have more than one Self, and possess upwards to a dozen different versions of it. For social psychologists, these concepts are roughly equated to the "I" and the "Me."

Damasio presents Core Self and Autobiographical Self to make these distinctions, but in common, the various disciplines acknowledge the fundamental manner in which we construct and perceive our individual identities. Different word choices across disciplines now offer a converging set of constructs which are helping create a common understanding of Self, Soul, Subject, and you and me.

A final comment from Lakoff and Johnson about morality: "One of the major findings of this empirical research is that our cognitive unconscious is populated with an extensive system of metaphoric mappings for conceptualizing, reasoning about, and communicating our moral ideals." (290) Our moral metaphor system is experientially grounded.

"Another striking finding is that the range of metaphors that define our moral concepts is fairly restricted (probably no more than two dozen basic metaphors)…" (290, 291)

These metaphors are all related to our well being: health, being strong, nurturing, freedom, being in control, and other similar constructs. "Morality is fundamentally seen as the enhancing of well-being, especially that of others." (291)

Morality is grounded in the most fundamental and also limited constructs created by our minds. These constructs are universal to our species. Using the language of complexity theory, they are mind emergents. Morality comes from within our psyches and is an integral part of who we are. From the point of view of my own intra-psychic experiential probes, the Moral Law is built into the algorithm of our DNA. It is hard to imagine any sentient species capable of creating advanced civilizations without this capacity. The Intelligent Universe does seem intelligent after all.

Moral metaphors are bound together by our culture, and can be interpreted to mean just my clan or tribe, my nation, or all humanity. We express moral empathy when we project our Self and become the other, or feel commiseration with others. We can reverse this role and feel the other's empathy projected onto our own self. Neural science tells us that when we subjectively feel what others are feeling, our brain duplicates the chemistry as well as the feeling and emotion of the person with whom we are sharing laughter, depression, or other emotions. If our friend is feeling sad, we come to feel sad, and thereby duplicate what their brain, brain chemistry, and mind is expressing. This basic mechanism of projection is bound up in our shared neural capacities which are based on the metaphorical Self – Cognitive Unconscious and the functioning of the neural networks in our brains that create mind and self.

THE SOUL ADRIFT

By externalizing reasoning, consciousness, and self as soul, we have failed to understand and empirically investigate our own religious nature, and failed to understand the biology of the brain. Consequently, we come to reject nature's (God's) design for the creation of a conscious, moral being capable of becoming a supportive partner in the Intelligent Universe. Thus, if one is a theist, we have failed and continue to fail in our fundamental knowledge of God by denying the basic design of our own minds and brains. If we are atheists, we fail to understand how the laws of nature are expressed in our own DNA by denying our religious nature.

Religious studies confirm time and again that we cannot study religious behavior by either assuming that our respective religious dogmas are correct, or by assuming that we can accept religious behavior at face value. Speaking-in-tongues is no longer a mystical phenomenon; spirit possession is no longer the work of spirits; out-of-body travel is no longer a trip to Heaven or Hell. And, visions are understood in this evolving scientific model as understandable constructions of our minds. The milieu of consciousness is also the milieu of ASC.

We come to understand that the uninformed theist is bedfellow with the uninformed atheist. They both share a common ignorance of humanity's basic religious nature, which resides in embodied self and Embodied Religion.

Quoting Damasio in *The Feelings of What Happens:* "The conscious mind and its constituent properties are real entities, not illusions, and they must be investigated as the personal, private, subjective experiences that they are." (308) All I have added to this most fundamental position of the neural scientist is that experiences of altered reality are one of these real properties even though they have been treated historically as coming from outside of our brains and bodies.

Reconciliation comes from empirical research of the Damasio and Lakoff-Johnson variety, where neural science and neural philosophy reveal the basic neural processes that go on in our brains. Failure to recognize how thought is created metaphorically, failing to recognize how sentient life forms emerge and evolve, or how our biological makeup creates consciousness, or how body serves as the primary grounding of metaphorical constructs necessary for thought and reasoning, all diminish human nature by denying our own capacities and directly ascribing them to the supernatural, or at a minimum, to some abstraction that is external to our bodies and minds.

The Cosmic Shaman's contribution to this developing understanding comes by removing the mysticism of altered reality experiences. I am arguing that traditional religion's existence has been predicated on hiding our true religious natures. Once we remove the mysticism of the mystic and the disembodied thoughts of super-naturalists, we are left with a new paradigm of Embodied Religion. Through this new model, we can explore our true religious nature and what this nature means in a natural universe or God's universe, and build on the legs of reason and science, both of which come from and are supported by our bodies and brains.

Tying this stream of thought together with the experiential psychology of altered realities, we acknowledge that all human thought, reasoning, and experiences, including religious ones, are subject to research. We can create, direct, and control the core elements of shamanic experiences, which utilize and express the same altered realities in world religions, as I've explained my own experiences in *Autobiography of a Ghost.* An embodied understanding of religion is a must if we wish to use our religious nature for the betterment of humanity and a meaningful future in our universe, whatever that future may be.

In *Mind of the Mystic,* I am inviting the reader to duplicate any altered reality common to history and world religions: astral travel, reincarnation, speaking in tongues, spirit possession, or spirit projection. Ability to duplicate research methodology in a controlled fashion, especially subjecting altered states of reality to neurologically advanced technology puts religion and religious studies on a plane with neural philosophy.

In contrast to Embodied Religion, altered realities that conform to accepted schema are seen as coming from and articulating with our prescribed religious dogmas. Altered realities that are generated by the same neural processes are rejected when they do not conform to established religious dogma, even when existing dogma is riddled with its own contradictions. What has happened with neural science, neural philosophy, neural linguistics, developmental psychology, and their related research technologies is the unveiling of how humanity becomes conscious, thinks, feels, reasons, and comes to experience reality, and taking the next step, how humanity creates and becomes conscious of altered realities.

Convergence of various scientific disciplines has gradually eroded the power base of world religions and subjected them to the light of creation. The challenge to traditional religion is: shall it remain in conflict with itself, or will it join science in an open and honest exploration of our divine nature. This divine nature is not a supposed and often defined corrupt nature that identifies others as enemies, or people who need to be wiped off the face of this planet and hence, subject to our swords. Rather, our divine nature can join the rest of humanity as brothers and sisters to achieve peace, harmony, and a livable world civilization; a civilization that earns the right to become part of an Intelligent Universe. Denying our own God-given or nature-given self, depending on your interpretation, has been at the center of the conflict between religion and science. It need not be!

THE SOCIOLOGIST'S ERROR

The sociologist's historical model of reality, which assumed that the mind was *sui generis,* unique, and *tabula rasa,* a blank slate, at birth cannot be correct. The neural sciences have shattered this assumption, and the pieces are too minute ever to be reassembled. Clearly we are discovering that our minds emerge from the same neural structures that have supported evolutionary development in species that have preceded Homo sapiens. A qualitative difference emerges as stages of consciousness and self come into being as described by neural science.

Further, as we come to understand what consciousness is and how it too emerges, it becomes impossible to ignore the meaning of how the neural structures in human development are assembled, and how this process occurs universally across humankind. Tabula rasa does not exist in the human psyche; the new born are not just blank slates waiting to be shaped by culture.

Culture cannot take on any form. Culture must express itself within the limits of human capacity, and culture for you and me is not relative. Culture makes a significant contribution to content from all perspectives, and the perspective of altered realities acknowledges this contribution. But universal neural capacity provides structure and direction to our developmental potential.

Failure of mainstream sociology to recognize the contributions of experimental psychology and the neural sciences has had disastrous consequences for many areas of human development. This is especially true in crime and punishment. One size fits all in the sociologist's Standard Model has filled American prisons to overflowing as the corner from the Twentieth to the Twenty-first Century was turned. Ignoring our human nature has been a disaster which calls for major corrections in sociological thinking.

Neural Philosophy adds to the sociologist's dilemma by demonstrating through testable hypotheses how thought is formed and comes to support human reasoning. The concept of self in Neural Philosophy is compatible with the neural sciences as both are based on empirical research, not just arm chair speculation that has often been given equal status with research-based science in sociology. A casual perusal of Andrew and Bonta's discussion of sociological theory in *The Psychology of Criminal Conduct,* and its disastrous impact on America's correctional system, provides a good example of the small box American sociologists have lived in.

Finally, reifying concepts of society and culture has been a bad sociologist's habit. Religion as a social institution, which simply means a complex pattern of social behavior and interaction created within one's culture, lets the sociologist study religion devoid of the human experience, devoid of human capacity, and devoid of all the complex neural machinery developed over millions of years of human evolution. Converging interdisciplinary research no longer permits this isolation from the rest of the world of science.

Consilience of the E. O Wilson variety begs students of various sciences to rub elbows, and in doing so, we discover links to our inner self, our nature, our biology, and our DNA. Sociobiology attempts to correct much of what has been inadequate in mainstream sociology. And I am not referring to the simple notion of sociobiology where the critic assumes our genes somehow express themselves directly in life. Rather, I am referring to a deeper sense of sociobiology where we conscientiously explore how the algorithms in our DNA come to be expressed. And in the discovery process, we find that neural structures stemming from our DNA create mind, consciousness, and self in a natural, knowable manner. Creating constructs beyond the human body and brain, reifying them in sociology in a manner that ignores the core element, you and me, misleads rather than leads our understanding of self, religion and society.

The lesson, I believe, of the shaman or mystic is that we must always ground every aspect of human creation in our minds, brains and bodies. Culture and society originate within our flesh and blood. We have moved over the past few thousand years from spirits causing illness to real world culprits such as bacteria causing illness. We have moved from use of the philosophical mind to explain all phenomena, to the creation of a multitude of scientific fields that actually accomplish this feat. We have moved from a speculative philosophy using reified constructs to explain everything from consciousness, to self, to research-based neural sciences that actually accomplish this task by honoring the same scientific methods that have worked so well in fields from physics to organic chemistry.

As the last bastions of the real mystics in our cultured world collapse, such as traditional religions, and non-research based philosophy and sociological speculation, we come face-to-face with humankind's last holdout: religion.

As a trained sociologist and social psychologist with strong concentrations in psychology and anthropology, I struggled as a young university professor to explain consciousness, ASC, and self. I did not have current knowledge from the neural sciences, but I did have experiential self experiments to guide me. I used a model from Symbolic Interaction that I modified, the symbolic self in relationship to what it referred to – the referential self.

Damasio made so much sense to me when I replaced referential self with embodied self. Referential-embodied self had to exist in my experience of ASC, or I could not explain the phenomena. Unfortunately, all of my lecture notes were lost in a flood almost thirty years ago, and I now must reconstruct these ideas from memory. Nevertheless, the fit is there, and I think contributes to an awareness that insight from the inside-out contributes to our understanding of these phenomena. However, these insights were not acceptable to the mental health community in the late 1950s through the 1970s, and often times thereafter. It is my sense that there is a meaningful convergence of disciplines operating now that will find some of these thoughts worthwhile. At least, it has been this assumption that has prompted me to put these words on paper.

9 - MONOTHEISM AND POLYTHEISM

CORRUPUTING HARMONY

Jonathan Kirsch, in *God Against The Gods,* provides a historical review of monotheism's rise to world religious power and its related suppression of polytheism. The invention of monotheism is attributed to Akhenaton, Egypt's pharaoh and absolute ruler, in the fourteenth century B.C.E. This is the world's first historical documentation of monotheism, and it being imposed top-down by a powerful ruler. Kirsch states: "...no idols were fashioned in the image of Aton, because, remarkably, he was a god whose form could not be imagined." (25) Akhenaton's experiment ended after seventeen years with his death, and Egypt returned in the main to its polytheistic ways.

Kirsch intimates that Moses might have been a priest of the Sun God, but at the least, seems to have borrowed many monotheistic ideas from the movement. Most importantly, concerning the idea of absolute power, he refers to Moses' "death squad," when Moses comes down from the mountain and kills three thousand innocent followers, including women and children, for worshipping false idols. Acts of this nature I have referred to throughout this book as belonging to the True Believer. I make this attribution because I can't imagine mass murder on this scale; murder of one's own tribal people because

127

belief is being taken casually. I also can't imagine killing one child for the same reason.

Kirsch references the Book of Exodus as it challenges the pharaoh of Egypt: "Who is Yahweh, that I should obey his voice?" a bemused pharaoh asks Moses. "I know not Yahweh." This is the standard interpretation in the stream that becomes contemporary Christianity. Kirsch continues: "The diggings at Tell el-Amarna, some 180 miles south of modern Cairo, tell a very different tale. Moses was not a strict monotheist. "Who is like you, O Yahweh, among the gods? I bless thee by Yahweh, and by his Asherah." (From an archaeological site in the Sinai by Kuntillat 'Ajrud. (Kirsch, 31) The Old Testament borrows heavily from Akhenaton without giving credit. Modern Christianity forgets the Asherah – God's partner.

Additionally, L. C. Schneider, Professor of Theology, Ethics, and Culture at Chicago Theological Seminary, in *Beyond Monotheism,* references the shared divine nature between Yahweh and the Persian One-God Ahura-Mazda during the time the Judeans are in Babylonian captivity, and then provides a clear historical review of Judaism's gradual transition from a polytheistic religion to monotheism. Yahweh was not the first One-God, and the growth of monotheism in Judaism's history is now well documented in streams of historical influence that represent complexity and diversity, which gradually became massaged into a dogmatic seamless whole by Emperor Constantine and the Church of Rome.

Kirsch makes a strong argument that the growth of Judaism's monotheistic worldview was not an easy accomplishment for Moses, and those who followed him. Polytheism displayed strong attachment to the human heart and was not fully put down in the West until Roman Emperors and The Church brought the full weight of the sword to bear. Constantine, like his polytheistic nemesis, Julian, claimed divine visions. Constantine also supported the Christian belief of demons. This belief keeps surfacing as we acknowledge The Church dusting off old rituals in these modern times, to rid their followers of similar possessions. Constantine supported the Christian idea that epilepsy was caused by demons, and not the emerging alternative "empirical" view. His life reflects that of one who covers his bases with appropriate gods at critical times.

Tribal mentalities dominated the ancient world as immature egos ruled through the sword, and the sword became the idol that determined common worship. Monotheists lived in a world populated by evil spirits as much as polytheists did, and the Lord of the Jews became a jealous, avenging God bent on keeping his people separate from the Gentiles. How could it be otherwise? Once exclusivity is claimed, and our group is set against all others, human nature keeps experiencing its special relationship with its own nature. Everything outside of the One-God is defined as evil, and this evil lurks behind every bush and closed door. Exclusivity of the One-God became the political organizing concept central to Judaism. This organizing force we understand well, with the spread of Euro-centrism and its historical colonial outreach.

I believe that the neural sciences along with psychology and other empirically-based sciences are confirming the innate source of our internal religious nature. Further, this algorithm in our DNA is expressed in the modern world as it has been expressed and documented countless times from ancient records to modern ethnographies. "Monotheism" denies that our religious nature is internal and substitutes dogma. Ironically, this singular striving toward oneness and unity is suppressed in the name of Oneness. Origins are the same for Islam, Christianity, and Judaism in this respect as the sword was used to achieve religious dominance, however, questions remain regarding Akhenaton's abstract concept of monotheism and how often he used the sword as pharaoh to impose his will. The rise of Persia's super-state power in the ancient world is much better documented and understood.

The historical and worldwide drive to reinterpret monotheistic religions reflects our human nature as expressed by shamans from Solomon, Moses, Jesus, Peter, and Paul, to the green jungles of Brazil, and the iron jungles of Los Angeles. I refer to these historical figures as shamans because they talked like and reported experiences as shamans. As we scan history, the voice of the shaman is found wherever we touch what is called sacred, supernatural, the other side, recall visions, become possessed by spirits, or cast out demons.

Our humanity demands expression of that which is central to consciousness and self. Neural sciences and psychology reveal this nature, and they increasingly unveil the origin of consciousness and self. I am stating rather unequivocally that shamanic experiences are at the core of all religious expression, and that historical documentation that can no longer be destroyed or confined by major world religions, supports this expression in religions both shamanic polytheism and monotheism.

The prophets of antiquity shared this divine visioning experience. They sought the sacred, felt the sacred, and shared the sacred, and were moved to ecstasy and revelation as shamans both then and now. How could it be otherwise? Our neural structure, minds and brains, are built upon the same DNA. Often we look at the forest of shamanic experiences and see only a few leafs, twigs, and trunks. When we look at the forest whole, we see not only individual trees, but the beauty, colors, and softness that provide comfort, refuge, and purpose. We see healers, social workers, and keepers of cultural traditions. Gods and goddesses speak to us in dreams, but our soul speaks to us in the Now. Collective Oneness, unity, wholeness, and integration provide the aliveness of being that brings joy and rapture.

Neanderthals burial practices and art reflect the autobiographical self, and a modern level of consciousness as revealed by the contemporary neural sciences. This is a neural capacity that lets us experience a timeless universe, something beyond our self, as well as the ability to model all of nature in the evolving memories of our minds. As we increasingly come to understand our own capacities through science, we see the world, our history, and our prophets through glasses of fading color and ever clearer imagery. Historical "god-like" figures that practice shamanic rituals are, in truth, reflecting a quintessential part of our DNA. Our humanity lies deep within.

Kirsch makes a strong case for human progress being equaled between polytheists and monotheists. The Jewish God of the Bible demands Abraham slay Isaac and offer the corpse on the altar fire. (Genesis 22:13). The roots of human cruelty grow deep into human history in terms of sacrifice. It is impossible to claim moral superiority on the part of monotheism when we recall its history. And, I might add, it is impossible to claim moral superiority on the part of theism versus atheism as the nurtured human heart beats in resonance with every other human heart. It shares the same Self, Soul, biological history and DNA.

"By 97 B.C.E., when the Roman Senate formally adopted a law that criminalized the offering of human victims, animal sacrifice had long before replaced the offering of human flesh and blood to the gods and goddesses of Greece and Rome," says Kirsch. (54) And, referencing the pagan emperor on the ideal pagan ruler, Julian says: "one who is just, kind, humane, and easily moved to pity" and one who champions "the poor against those who are strong, dishonest, and wicked." (Ibid) We find compassion, love, and understanding not in polytheism or monotheism, but rather in the human heart unfettered by exclusive dogma. I would add that it is found in human nature, and that it is the expression of our human nature that creates, always creates, the complexity of religious expression. This is what Schneider calls multiplicity.

Again, my favorite historical supporter of religious freedom is Genghis Khan. The Great Sky that covers all of us permits each one of us to worship as he or she chooses. The Great Khan recognized our inherent religious nature as he experienced it himself, and decreed religious freedom throughout his conquered territories. Polytheistic conqueror that he was, he established religious freedom in the world's largest historical empire; a freedom that was taken aback by subsequent rulers, including those of the West when his empire was fragmented and went into decline. A simple man was the Khan, and I don't mean simple in the sense of being cognitively limited; simple in the sense of pureness of spirit that recognized our innate human right to be who we are: Homo religiosus.

Glen A. Just

SHAMANS ARE ONE SIZE

Failure to define the shaman and shamanism has led to a plethora of conundrums. One need only peruse the findings of the International Society for Shamanistic Research to experience lack of agreement as to what shamans and shamanism are. I will use the proceedings of the Sixth Biannual Conference held in Estonia in August of 2001 as examples. Personally, as the "Cosmic Shaman," I think the definitions are fairly easy, but will save them for later after a few paragraphs of reflection.

True Believers, I define as those ethnographers who see shamanic experiences being guided by a hidden supernatural hand. Referencing Marjorie Mandelstam Balzer in Sakha, where she reports: "I started near my hearth, dressed in [traditional] clothing and using a drum I had made myself. I did not know what would come of it, but I started beating on the drum and chanting. Soon two beings, exactly, definitely two, appeared on either side of me. I did not know what to think. I even asked myself 'Am I normal?' Most shamans are perhaps abnormal, so the thinking of many people and some scientists goes. But this is just an illusion. My mind was sound. My logic was intact. Indeed, I am always psychologically healthy. More than most. So I looked and I saw I was very far from my hearth. I was recending, and I came into the house of the man who had insulted me. He was very frightened. I am not sure what I or the spirits did. The next day I came to him in person. He looked at me in horror. I laughed and walked out. To this day, when I see him, he turns away. We do not greet each other." (Barkalaja, 37)

Fieldwork and publications on shamanism are riddled with similar reports. I am hopefully clear throughout this book that altered states of consciousness (ASC) are strict reflections of cognitive-emotional mechanisms that emerge from flesh and blood. My emphases on neural science, biology, and psychology as revealers of the mechanics behind ASC are stressed to make the point. Read the proceedings from one of these international conferences and you will find those who believe in science rubbing elbows with those who believe in magic (see Leete and Firnhaber.)

Anzori Barkalaja attempts the incorporation of Antonio Damasio's work into his discussion of shamanism. He notes that Damasio integrates self and consciousness into the body state as a whole, but Barkalaja does not develop working concepts of neural science or use them to enlarge understanding of the shaman or shamanism. He further states that, "Damasio has attempted to explain the questions of mind, mentality and soul through neurobiological mechanisms only, which however, rules out the truth value of the shaman's personal experience as a reality." (37) One step into the world of empirical science and one step out: score = zero. "Truth value," what does Barkalaja mean by this? Is there a truth that comes from "beyond?" Is there a truth that exists in the nether world of the shaman's experiences that represents communication with immortals from the supernatural? I read him as writing with the latter intent. Clarity, however, demands more.

Barkalaja: "Thus shamanism is not something that exists by itself as a phenomenon or as a method. Shamanism could possibly become a research area of shamanhood that concerns the boundary wherein the means available to science could provide the opportunity for writing into the overall human information design, our own lines, in order to mark the point of convergence with the 'indescribably' through the disjunctive chain of association of the texts of scientific paradigm." (50)

Now I must be unkind: Does he mean that shamanism can be studied scientifically, and in these studies we can find where the shaman's experiences articulate the sacred and secular? If not, then I find the word game tiring. Let us not wrap the language of science around the musings of historical, religious philosophers. Science demands that we state relationships clearly, operationalize our concepts through methodolgies that can be duplicated, and clearly state the causative linkages. He does not.

Perhaps I am being overly critical of Barkalaja; nevertheless, I appreciate his efforts to join science with studies of shamanism, but I think we can do better than this. I will provide a few more quotes to make my point.

Glen A. Just

Barkalaja: "Thus, it is possible that the shaman or any person engaged in a creative activity, processes information through the visual centre." (44)

Barkalaja: "… there is a need for a unifying theory that would direct scientific investigation and allow for connections with other disciplines. This theory must draw upon a predominately etic method, because this is the only form that can be proved falsifiable in cases of theoretical analysis." (31) Generally, we mean by etic that one does not participate in the culture being studied.

Barkalaja referencing (Narby 1999): "Jeremy Narby has offered an interesting line of reasoning concerning the potential direction of a new theory by showing possible connections between DNA and ASC. What Narby discusses is the relationship between the length of a DNA double helix and the shaman's axis mundi: "Shamans say that the axis mundi is very long, so long that it connects the earth and heaven." (Narby 17) Narby refers to DNA as a kind of text, "There's a symbolic unity underlying all of nature." (ibid)

Cause and effect relationships require us to connect DNA and ASC. We cannot support our hypothesis indirectly or obliquely. Innuendo, by association, continues to build a mystic framework through word manipulation. What is the mechanism of "myth as information design?" We cannot just talk about concepts and the relationship between concepts, scientific process requires that the concepts be made operational. Barkalaja cannot recover credibility by championing a new interdisciplinary approach without being more explicit. Is there a deep seated code in DNA that supports and nourishes life, as he speculates? Does life on earth depend on the Sun? Are the heavy elements of the Cosmos created in supernova? The answer is yes! We cannot just repeat what is tested by science and cloud these findings in words of association while claiming new insight or wisdom, or we remain in a shamanic trance.

Barkalaja: "The appearance of anthropological shamanism is an attempt to bring elements of a traditional worldview into the positivistic Western worldview." (26)

I disagree as most anthropological fieldwork is of an ethnographic design and remains outside of interdisciplinary cooperation. Although this international conference was a serious attempt to connect the two, it did so without articulating a design for interrelationships, and never defined its basic subject matter, the shaman and shamanism. He goes on to talk about "urban shamanism," and, "neo-shamanism," and introduces further ideas about information design. However, his best work and comments come from the field as he observes and reports on the shaman's world. Methodology of fieldwork does not permit him to summarily reject rigorous methodological findings of neural scientists like Antonio Damasio. If he rejects Damasio's "hard science" that explains consciousness and self empirically, he is required to tell us why. We have much interdisciplinary communication begging to be addressed. Calling for interdisciplinary collaboration demands greater and clearer reciprocity, and it must include the natural sciences and specified use of related methodolgies.

Barkalaja:"I realize more and more fully that the methods used by shamans are based upon the entire range of mechanisms that humans make use of." (49)

And mountains rise above the sea, and in their prominence cast shadows unto the beaches of our lives, I say. Shamans are humans like you and me, not minor gods. And, yes, they do profess contact with the supernatural.

Shamans and shamanism emerge from this conference and are published in a non-critical text that still leaves the reader with multiple "visions." Shamans come in so many shapes and sizes; shamans can be in various states of ecstasy, out-of-body travelers, healers, controller of spirits, originators of myth, preservers of culture, devils who eat their own children, and the list becomes almost endless. Is there a model, paradigm, or organizational framework to guide ethnography and research? I suggest that the dilemma resides in conflicting worldviews of the natural and the supernatural; science and superstition as they are randomly mixed together. This separation must be addressed for a scientific model of study to emerge.

Ake Hultkarantz refuses to define shamanism but attempts to define the shaman. "A shaman is a social figure who, with the help of assisting spirits reaches ecstasy for communicating with

the supernatural world in the interests of his group members."
(Hultkarantz 1973:34) This limitation of defining the shaman
continues the focus on ecstasy states which are quite common to
many aspects of chronicled ethnographies, but the definition is
not comprehensive enough.

Anna-Leena Siikala defines character of the shaman's
actions: "The technique of communication used by a shaman as
a creator of state of interaction between this world and the other
world is fundamentally an ecstatic role taking-technique."
(Siikala 1987: 28) Siikala selects the "ecstatic role taking-
technique" for her focus. This represents a selective process of
picking and choosing, acts that are common to this conference;
one that does not reach a level of generalization upon which a
comprehensive model can be built. Speaking-in-tongues is a
compatible ecstatic role taking-technique. However, shamanic
flights, for example, are not ecstatic yet employ similar
mechanisms to communicate with the "other side. We can do
better than this.

Barkalaja (35) on Arnold Ludvig: "The conception of ASC
as defined by Arnold Ludvig encompasses all the states of
consciousness outside the normal waking state, "including day
dreams, sleep and dream states, hypnosis, sensory deprivation,
hysterical states of dissociation and depersonalization, and
pharmacologically-induced mental aberrations." (Siikala
1987:32)
Now Barkalaja has my attention, however, I want him to sort
out these different offerings and make them into a coherent
whole. Why doesn't he take the next step?
I have been, perhaps, too critical with works and comments
of those who like myself seek answers to the shaman and
shamanism, answers which are not always easy to come by.
Point made, nevertheless, is our need to remove this confusion
so we can combine research findings into a "standard model"
that does more than repeat findings from field experiences and
thereby maintains the conflict that I experience between those
who attempt to explain the shaman and shamanism with

reference to both the supernatural and the natural, thereby mixing the two.

One last reference to the 6th biannual Conference of the International Society for Shamanistic Research: Jeremy Narby dabbles in mind-altering drugs in the Brazilian jungle, and then takes three other individuals back and subjects them to the same mind altering drug trip that he had earlier experienced (see Narby). I give him credit for attempting to help each of these individuals discover new knowledge that is not available to our normal consciousness. He reports the effects of each drug trip and leaves the reader with the impression that some connection has been made with knowledge from the "other side," as it is similarly understood by the locals. Narby demonstrates two things: He lacks understanding of hallucinogenic drugs and their effects, and he perpetuates the idea that "truth" resides in an external consciousness. I predict that a more complete explanation for the neuro-chemical mechanisms behind ASC will not be kind to this type of field reporting.

DEFINING THE SHAMAN AND SHAMANISM

Point 1: Polytheists and monotheists are both reflecting our biological nature.

Point 2: Both polytheists and monotheists create a supernatural world that is external to the self, and they do so by fashioning an intra-psychic, culturally dependent worldview built from altered states of consciousness.

Point 3: Conflict between polytheists and monotheists historically has continued into the present era, and this conflict obscures scientific research into our religiosity.

Point 4: Interdisciplinary research, with psychology and the neural sciences, which plays a key role in our analysis, is beginning to explain consciousness and self.

Point 5: The emerging model of consciousness and self is also offering fundamental insight into altered states of consciousness.

Point 6: Altered states of consciousness are being documented as employing the same biochemical and neurological mechanisms as normal states.

Point 7: Altered states of consciousness create a range of experiences that have been historically interpreted as putting our normal state of consciousness in contact with the supernatural. (We now understand this process as self talking to self.)

Point 8: Explaining altered states of consciousness is fundamental to understanding normal states of consciousness, and combining this information permits us to comprehend what is going on in the mind of the shaman (mystic is my term.)

Point 9: Explaining the mechanism behind ASC explains the shaman's experience both in tribal and world religions.

Point 10: Understanding the shamans experience permits us to define shamanism and other forms of religious experience. Defining the shaman and shamanism becomes possible through the use of scientific findings in the natural sciences: neural science, psychology and medicine. When we explain ASC visions and experiences, and when we duplicate and control them at will; we can bring the entire analysis into the laboratory, and subject this analysis to modern technology. This does not obsolete field work and the historical or ongoing efforts to document shamanic expressions around the world. Anthropology and sociological fieldwork is to be respected in its own right. However, this level of analysis, devoid of the natural sciences, does not answer our most fundamental questions related to definition. And without definition, we circle the subject endlessly when we could be creating greater clarity.

Altered states of consciousness are part of our biological makeup. Shamans come in one size, and shamanic figures behind world religions are no longer exempt from this analysis. Religious power and size does not make a hands-off exclusiveness acceptable. Knowledge of our religious nature is knowledge of self, is knowledge of where we have come from, and where we will go. It is too precious to leave in boxes of mystification.

I have referenced Barbara Wilhelmi because we both arrive at the same conclusions about shamans. She sees biblical figures as shamans much as I do. Walk like a duck, talk like a duck, as the saying goes, and you are a duck. I do not mean to put-down historical religious figures, as they represent the same capacities and yearnings that I experience in myself and others. But I do contend that we are obligated to use the same definitions and findings of science in an objective analysis of the data. Religion cannot continue to be exempt from science.

The shaman is any individual who practices altered states of consciousness within a cultural worldview that assumes the existence of a supernatural plane of reality. Not all shamans practice ASC across its full range of expression. Some may focus on ecstasy, others on out-of-body movements, a few with speaking-in-tongues, etc. What is common to all is the activation of neural pathways that alter normal perception or sensory information processing. As I've pointed out elsewhere in this text and in *Autobiography of a Ghost,* ASC is the activation of "scrambled" neural networks. By scrambled I mean opening neural pathways to provide experiences outside of normal sensory processing. (I touch upon a number of potential mechanisms for these ASC experiences referencing Damasio and LeDoux in this book.) It is my contention that we must either document empirically what these mechanisms are, or in this stage of development, hypothesize what they are, and then move to the next step of empirical support or rejection.

Shamanism is the systematic use of ASC to make sense of the world and community inhabited by the practitioner that contributes to the development and maintenance of social order within their communities. Explaining ASC is part of this system of cultural definitions as ASC is a "normal" part of the brains functioning that creates consciousness. Cultures are composed of people struggling to make meaning of their worlds. Hence, shamanism may be viewed as a broad practice, much like the general practitioner MD. Shamanic practices do and must deal with the broad range of human issues from physical sickness to mental illness, to plagues, wars and droughts. I not only have no need to mystify the shaman but think that fieldwork that maintains this mystification is misleading. Consistently, I have maintained that interdisciplinary research is necessary and it must be empirically verifiable.

Glen A. Just

You might ask why I have referred to myself as a shaman, in fact the Cosmic Shaman. I came by ASC naturally as many shamans do; in my case, as the result of suffocation by my mother. My personal history has carved a path through most states of ASC, and I have pointed out in *Ghost* the steps of discovery and eventual explanations for these experiences. I have practiced ASC most of my life, and my experiences are part of this analysis. However, this is only my second attempt to act as a shaman in the sense of using it to explain a beginning framework for an alternative view of religion and our religious nature. You decide!

I have stated repeatedly that ASC must be documented scientifically if we wish to more fully understand our own humanness. It must be understood if we are to avoid using religion to abuse ourselves or others, and it must be scientifically explored if we are ever to understand the hidden codes in this Intelligent Universe. And that is not mystical at all.

JEWS, CHRISTIANS AND MOSLEMS

Major world religions have grown out of our religious nature as expressed by shamanic practices and abilities. Personally, I think it is impossible to explore our religious history without this awareness repeatedly hitting us over the head. We seek the love of a mate because that is an inherent part of our DNA, part of our perpetuation as a species. We seek explanations for ASC because it is an inherent component of our consciousness and expression of self. Power corrupts, as the saying goes, and absolute power corrupts absolutely, in both the sacred and secular. Let us substitute reason and an understanding of our own religious nature as we move to eliminate this corruption from the misuse of religion.

Barbara Wilhelmi writes that "Only a few Christian theologians use the word shamanism. A closer look reveals that shamanic practices are in no way uniformly rejected in the texts of the New Testament." (142) She then goes on to provide examples:

140

- Jesus in the wilderness fasting and fighting the Devil.
- Luke, 31:33: "I am driving out demons and performing cures." (To heal and exorcise was Jesus' disciple's mission as well, and they were successful as a movement in a demon-possessed land).
- (Mark 1, 12-13) "The special communication with wild animals and angels is also described." (145).
- (Mark, Ch.16) "… later there is a reference to 'picking up snakes.'" "This suggests the use of a specific ritual."
- Moses shamanic practices (see Num 12, 13) Moses draws a circle and asks for healing. (146)
- "Thus, Jesus is said to have used a well-known healing formula talitha kumi, saliva, and also drawing of circles in the sand." (146)
- "Thus also Peter heals with the phrase talitha kumi."
- "Origins specifically defend the Christian belief in demons as opposed to the rational diagnosis of epilepsy." (see Kollman 1996:374)

This is not a critique of Christianity. Schneider does this infinitely better than I do; I merely want to emphasize the shamanic origin of world faiths. I have used the expression regarding shamans that one size fits all. Shamanic practices are shamanic practices, and activate "normal" neural-chemo mechanisms common to each one of us. Religion is not that hard to understand once we come to know the workings of our own minds through science, and I maintain that the next level of religious awareness is even more awe-inspiring than that of our "pastoral" ancestors.

Diversity of religious practices historically reflects greater self unity through polytheism than rigid monotheism because it represents the God within: Homo religiosus. When we come to appreciate the religious nature each of us holds within, we can acknowledge why our ancestors expressed this nature in such a multiple number of ways. It is an Oneness of origin: a multiplicity of expressions. In this respect, polytheism is closer to the truth of human nature than how monotheism has been practiced when it denies the God within us. We enter the age of science by finally wresting monotheism from Moses' extended death squads. With greater historical accuracy, we wrestle the sword of monotheism from the dead hands of Akhenaton or Ahura-Mazda.

As we come full circle back to our biological, religious nature, we strip away any rationale that permits killing those who hold different beliefs. The True Pagan is you and me, and the paradox becomes: Rigorous, fundamental interpretations of monotheism raise the sword that kills with religious fervor and passion. Theism within each of these historical religious expressions can find our humane nature once we mature enough personally and socially to realize the full potential in our DNA.

RELIGION AND SCIENCE RECONCILED

History reveals a different understanding of contemporary monotheism, and I think reasonable evidence exists to establish monotheism's growth out of shamanism. They are bedfellows in the sense that their mother/father comes from the same human capacity in our DNA. This awareness helps us appreciate our religious nature, and directly raises questions for the hardcore atheist.

Christianity has been remade in the modern world by ignoring the Bible's angry God and focusing on its loving God, thereby reflecting the emergence of a new world that truly reflects the God within each one of us. Science, reason, and cultural progress will have it no other way. The extremists in Islam, Christianity, and Judaism have yet to reconcile their differences by letting go of their historical intolerance. Slogans of insight: Kill an abortion doctor for Christ; kill an Infidel for Allah; kill a Moslem for Yahweh. Science has and is playing a central role in helping create a world where we are fed, clothed, and housed adequately, and from this support level, achieve greater realization of the humane potential programmed within each of us. This support level has traditionally been a key political doctrine in socialism, which harks back to a key idea within a number of early Christianities. We are obligated as one world people to bring this level of support to all children and all families. Until we do, body explosives or their equivalent will continue to detonate.

The God within supports human development to become the God without, thereby creating a world of harmony, mutual human respect, and strivings to end our historical madness. The world of "isms" collapses with the fruits of science when we create a world order based on mutual respect and rational planning dedicated to healthy children, families, and communities. The ghost of communism for America is just a ghost. Socialism is not a dirty word. The worshippers of Allah are our neighbors, and democracy becomes more than a slogan when it discovers how to provide for all its citizens.

Firnhaber attempts to reconcile science and shamanism by proposing a five level ASC map (100). "Recognizing that neurophysiological change is at the core ASC, research is beginning to include the pure science of the neurochemical dimensions of the phenomenon, consequently neurologist, neurobiologist, chemists, and medical researchers are now contributing to the scenario." (85) I believe his attempt squarely addresses a major goal in our study of shamanism. However, I will take a few paragraphs to address his concluding thoughts in this article: "Mapping the ASC: A Cultural-Physiological Construct" (84-99):

"a) If neurochemistry is all there is, what of mystery?" (98).

Answer: We do not ask in the area of disease when scientific explanations replace demons and spirits, "what of mystery." We look back and rejoice at the new world that opens to us. It is a healthier world, a world made less painful and frightening; a step in the direction of utopia, if you will. Mystery looms eternally on humankind's foreseeable future. Fear resides in ignorance, and ignorance does not fully know mystery; ignorance only experiences mystery. As Damasio says about our consciousness, we are not only conscious, but conscious of being conscious. In similar fashion: We not only appreciate each new mystery, but are conscious of this appreciation. Shall we not strive to attain the next higher level of consciousness?

Glen A. Just

"c) Must we redefine the nature of ordinary, sensory constructed, consensus reality?" (99)

The answer is yes, we must redefine the nature of reality, individual or consensus constructed reality. Failure to define ASC reflects our ignorance of consciousness and consciousness' alternate side, ASC. Reality constructions based on false premises such as the "other side" speaking to me through hallucinogens, consensus or not, must go. These are drug trips in the jungle just as certainly as they are drug trips taken by the gurus of LSD. Consensus reached about the shamans behind monotheisms of Egypt, Israel, Rome, or Mecca are now called into question.

"d) Can studies in the relationship between physiological and cultural experiences of every sort lead us to heightened insights into the nature of spirituality, religion, transcendence and their roles and requirements for human beings?" (99)

Again, the answer is yes, the nature of spirituality becomes clearer when we unveil the basic mechanisms of shamanism and our most fundamental religious experiences. Cultural consensus changes, but this has been the history of a species moving from human sacrifice to visions of travelling to the stars. The paradigm shift is enlightening, not frightening.

"e) Are their indicators in these studies that might impact other aspects of the human situation, healing, for example?" (99)

I have chronicled in *Ghost* my own healing process when I accessed the potential in my own consciousness, including the ASC component. I do not believe that I am unique. As we come to understand consciousness and ASC, we also understand mental health and social harmony from a new vantage point. The intra-psychic walls that block each of our psyches from being whole are torn down, and unity emerges in multiple forms – not a paradox at all.

[f] "And, perhaps the question of all questions: Where do we go in ASC? What, really, is it that we experience: Are we able to discuss these things at all?" (99) Firnhaber suggests: "… there is now the possibility of approaching and discussing these and other issues, that there are things that we can say about them, and that such discussion may become profoundly

important to us individually and collectively as we struggle with both the ontological and practical issues of our present moment in history." (99)

Answer: We experience intra-psychic phenomena during ASC. We can say endless things about these experiences, however, we must stop simply recording the multitude of ASC experiences and attach them to scientific interpretations. Through these attachments we arrive at explanation and understanding that does not emerge when mystification of knowable phenomena is maintained when we ignore interdisciplinary research.

Barbara Wilhelmi: "Not only could the Christian spiritual welfare and therapy practice be revitalized through this reconnection with the roots of Christianity." (148)

Wilhelmi sees the loss of Christianity's shamanic past as detrimental to its own movement as well as Christian ability to reconcile with other religions. I add to her thoughts by finding neglect of our shamanic abilities and related ASC misunderstandings detrimental to a core understanding of self and consciousness, thereby precluding a more comprehensive understanding of our religious nature – a nature shared across professed religions.

Recognizing that all humans have the capacity for normal and altered states of consciousness brings us back to Eden, and a common recognition that we are members of one family, cut from the same sacred cloth, searching for meaning and purpose in a world fragmented by word games of infinite design. Fortunately, this infinite design of confusion is slowly yielding to science and interdisciplinary research. This is truly a wonderful time to be a student of self, consciousness, shamanism, and religion as it moves us from pastoral barbarism to a realizable vision of world harmony, with the divisions between science and religion slowly dropping by the wayside. In the paradigm of Embodied Religion, it is without question that you and I are brothers and sisters. Welcome to my world.

10 - SCIENCE AND RELIGION CONVERGE

THE GLACIER MOVES

Ghost and *Mystic* demonstrate through experiential experiments that shamanic states associated with the mystic's spiritual contacts are intra-psychic phenomena. Self directed and controlled experiential experiments over fifty years has removed any doubt in my mind about psychic episodes we call astral travel, reincarnation, speaking-in-tongues, and the like, as they are unquestionably mind generated. They are not phenomena given us by the spirits or the gods, or God. Neural scientists such as Antonio Damasio address this subject briefly in *Looking for Spinoza*. I enjoyed Spinoza in the 1970's as a young professor, and found his religious philosophy to be surprisingly familiar. A God who was timeless, without form, and ubiquitous throughout the universe rang true to my own searching self at that time. I couldn't imagine a universal God having physical form or sitting on a throne, which had been my impression as a young child. A timeless, formless God was an abstract, but not too abstract, energy force permeating everyone and everything. This God was found within each one of us and was responsible for the ultimate identification of self with every particle and life form in the universe. This still works for me when I reach inside myself and feel this entity.

146

Support from neural science and neural philosophy increasingly provides insight into how the brain is creating consciousness, and constructing a sense of self, thereby helping return the subjectivity of historical religions to objective observation and experimentation. As a student of people sciences in the late 1950's and early 1960's, I did not have the luxury of using unobtrusive instruments to scan my brain. In fact, modern discussions by neural scientists about consciousness and "scrambled" neural pathways were out of the question fifty years ago. I simply experimented on my own and enjoyed the new paradigm as an audience of one. However, the world of science has not stood still, and the interdisciplinary convergence taking place is a joy to behold. It has also become an ever greater threat to established church dogmas and hierarchies, with repeated calls for the faithful to reject science and focus on belief. I think this is an error on the part of church notables, as truth will have its day. Mental giants like Galileo and Spinoza do not remain silent, and suppressing truth is equivalent to suppressing the human spirit, and freedom of thought cannot long be confined.

If I line up just a few of the historical myths in the monolithic edifice of Rome, or in the combined case of Catholicism and Judaism for Spinoza, the point is easily made. We are not the center of the universe, as planet Earth does circle the sun. Evolution is not blasphemy, but scientific fact. God is understood differently by various cultures, and does not neatly fit into the current interpretation of dogma in Rome, for example, the Ten Commandments are taken from the Egyptian Book of the Dead.

Monolithic churches keep adjusting their absolute but changing positions and interpretations as forced to do so by science. Perhaps this keeps larger numbers of believers donating regularly in any given time period, nevertheless, it does create both the alienated and the casual church participant. Large numbers of individuals attend church for fellowship and goodwill, not through blind acceptance of the dogma that is continuously being modified and reinterpreted as new knowledge of life and the universe is uncovered. Reconciliation of science and religion, which requires acceptance of scientific facts for those who let their minds roam free or explore their own religious nature, must become compatible if the world of science and religion are to ever embrace.

Neural Philosophy is demonstrating that the long and hard journey to understand how we construct thought and reason becomes clearer year by year. As we explore thought and reason from an empirical standpoint, continuing to assume that thought exists independent of our minds is no longer possible. Philosophers such as Descartes and Kant are taken to task for creating mystical externalized constructs that are assumed to exist independent of the human mind. Kant's "pure thought" made him a giant in Western Philosophy, until the neural sciences demonstrated that "pure thought" was impossible. Thought originates in the brain and body, and consciousness and self are possible because of the brain's constant use of the body as a reference.

Descartes, like Aristotle, separated mind and body, and his whole philosophy is based upon this assumption. A major icon of the Christian Church, Thomas Aquinas, is also a common bedfellow in this regard, and saw the jumbled thoughts of Aristotle as most of us perceive Aristotle in the modern world; as an organized whole. I do not mean to detract from either Aristotle or Aquinas, both of whom I enjoyed in their time, but in the context of the magnifying capacity of contemporary science, this edifice of Western Philosophy crumbles as a larger tower of wisdom emerges from the empirical sciences. The conflict is not with verifiable knowledge from the sciences. Rather, the conflict results from refusal to reconcile old religions, over decades or centuries, with new knowledge.

Tension between science and religion is exacerbated today by the increasing speed with which new knowledge is generated by the sciences. Slow moving changes of the 16th and 17th Centuries could be suppressed and held in check by The Church. This is no longer possible.

Traditional interpretations of God saw "Him" working His magic outside the brain and body in an odd version of mystical cyberspace. In light of science explaining how our brains work and how our minds emerge from brain and body, this older paradigm now seems rather strange. It continues to live through early childhood indoctrination. Whereas, a religion for all time and all people can be engaged at any age as it is compatible with science's discovery of nature's laws, or God's laws, if you choose.

The neural sciences are proposing rigorous models explaining consciousness and self that are increasingly being teased out with new technology, more specifically, a scanning, and tunneling religious quantum microscope of rigorous experiments. Convergence of multi-disciplinary approaches is progressively eroding the bedrock upon which the old gods stood. When we trace *Revolutions in Science* with Cohen, or *The Structure of Scientific Revolutions* with Kuhn, it is hard not to appreciate the historical difficulty of bringing new ideas to public acceptance and university perusal. Ideals that were easily proven, such as the Earth circling the Sun, were suppressed by the Church upon pain of death. Dogma was enforced by the sword until public education made it possible to exercise free thought, which depended upon shifts in power and control of the military made possible by the Industrial Revolution. Today the struggle is between free scientific inquiry and passionate indoctrination of dogma. Freeing the mind of magic is not easy.

Fortunately, today we are under little threat of death. The Grim Reaper of religion, except for radical aspects of Islam and Christian execution of abortion doctors, no longer threatens the death penalty for disagreement. Excommunication and ostracism are the chief tools of control in the 20th and 21st Centuries. However, battles won are sometimes battles later lost as with the anti-evolution movement in North America. Dogma, once established by numbers and political power, especially if political power can buy military might, is incredibly resistant to change as is evidenced by the history of The Church and its behavior before, during, and after the Inquisition.

Today, accepted models of externalized thought, ones that see God as an absolute, all powerful, timeless, and omnipresent entity independent of our brains and minds, is done with great difficulty. Our presence in this fine tuned universe, with its magically precise equations, with time that flows backwards and forwards, and a seemingly infinite amount of energy, acquires beauty and wonder through science that cannot be

Glen A. Just

matched by visions in the heads of our barely literate or illiterate shamans as they initially created world religions. Words cannot equal the beauty of visual reconstructions of DNA as it duplicates, and this wonder of scientific wonders never stops. Words without substance, such as God creating the world and man in six days and resting on the seventh, can only be taken literally with great effort. Fortunately, scientific findings from multiple fields are circling their wagons, and this time, dysfunctional thoughts are contained in the center. Scientific advances continue in biology, genetics, and evolution, and reason and consciousness becomes less mysterious in psychology and the neural sciences. The secrets of the universe are now revealed in physics and chemistry. Although progress in religion is slow, nevertheless, cracks are appearing everywhere as scientific knowledge slowly creeps into the public mind. Notice that I use public mind not as something external to each one of us, but as an extension of our collective awareness.

RELIGIOUS BY NATURE

I have added a lifetime of shamanic experiences and self experiments to the mix that explores the origin of religion and religion's basic assumptions. In an effort to explain my own history, I have searched through a broad swath of multiple study areas, and in doing so, have come to feel a commitment to help bring disembodied religion out of the closet. In my experience, the chief researchers shedding light on religious mysticism come from psychology and the neural sciences. As increasing numbers are exposed to higher education, whether they are university graduates or thoughtful non-university thinkers, and as we continue to gain knowledge about human development and functioning, there is an increase in tension with traditional religions and religion's houses of worship. An ever larger number of these modern seekers are forming their own churches and meeting places around the world, in order to express what I have presented as our DNA derived religious yearnings.

150

Consequently, waste is laid to the idea that one cannot be a good person, know God, or be saved unless they accept the current interpretation of dogmas that inevitably evolve with new understandings of history, and the advance of science.

Many individuals, me included, find it impossible to ignore our most fundamental inner self as we mature, age, and increase the depth of understanding that comes from science, history, and technology. I have not become religious in my elder years; I have always had a religious nature. I am like so many hundreds of thousands founding new organizations of worship from which fellowship and spirit can be shared along with common concerns, a sense of community, and a desire to create a better world.

Like so many others of similar persuasion, I have discovered my own religious nature, and find the fruit of religious dogma to be overripe. World religions are transforming themselves as part of this paradigm shift, and large numbers of Christian members in my experience no longer believe the model set forth by Constantine and the Church of Rome in 325 CE. They come to worship in the spirit of belonging and caring, not to save their souls, that reified, externalized, non-human form that floats in cyber space's equivalent. They come to purify their souls in acts of human kindness as they reach out to others, strive to save our environment, find communion returning beached mammals to the sea, or seek an endless number of means to bring harmony to this troubled planet. Spirit becomes a living force, not a ritual.

Putting our religious nature under the microscope brings surprising resonance with neural philosophy, the neural sciences, and developmental psychology. And from this analysis, I have set forth a number of hypotheses which are more fully laid out in the Epilogue. Peace has come to my youthful troubled mind by discovering the spirit that lives within, discovering my religious nature, bringing together the marvelous findings of science, and shedding the baggage of traditional dogma.

I do not wish to beat up on those who find similar peace within their own religious philosophies, but merely ask that freedom of religious thought be given to the rest of us. To quote

Glen A. Just

Damasio in *The Feeling of What Happens:* "We only create a sense of good and evil as well as norms of conscionable behavior once we know about our own nature and that of others like us." (315) Loss of innocence is not evil; evil is the hijacking of consciousness, self, and knowledge of our human nature, either God or nature given as the case may be.

Continuing with Damasio: "…in a variety of imperfect ways, individually and collectively, we have the means to guide creativity, and in so doing, improve human existence rather than worsen it." (316)

The wrapper of darkness that perpetuates human misery by denying rights of the affected from stem cell research, for example, is incompatible with our religious nature. It is only compatible with images of God created in bastions of ancient power. Can one really imagine the God who gave us our nature giving any socially created organization, major centers of world religious power, authority to deny medicine's right to stem cell research with all its potential to alleviate the misery of untold millions? Such a God would have denied us modern medicine altogether, and such a God would still have us slaughtering thousands at the foot of the mountain. Fortunately, that Yahweh is dead, as new Yahweh's have emerged over the last two thousand years.

Humanity acknowledges a religious nature not addressed by major world religions when these historical worldviews are set against science. The Moral Law, I am contending, has greater demonstrated effectiveness when it is acknowledged through personal expression than when it is promulgated through public piety. Waving a Bible on the street corner cannot compare with feeding a hungry child. Further, assuming that traditional forms of prayer that are of a ritual nature changes criminals is not supported, although carefully designed programs of cognitive restructuring derived from science are. Consistently, science keeps telling us that our God-given, or nature-given, capacities must be used to improve the human condition. The only loss I can perceive in recognizing that our religious nature is internal and not derived from some mystic demigod is to remove some of the direct control from traditional church hierarchies, and give it back to God or nature, depending on your perspective.

And if one is an atheist, it is simply recognized as a biological emergent which is part of our DNA. From either perspective, conflict is removed by recognizing commonalities between science and the new religious paradigm.

The Moral Law comes from an algorithm in our DNA; it is a biological emergent, much as Satinover argues in *The Quantum Brain*. Neural science, biology, psychology, and cultural analyses support this assumption. We emerge as a species, thrive, and grow multi-fold by helping others. Helping others is beneficial to ourselves, and increases our development on all fronts. Treating Moral Law as existing "out there," independent of our biology, permits its manipulation by powerbrokers and warlords, but treating the Moral Law as a natural human expression, regardless of how we see its source, holds us accountable for every human act. Nothing corrupt can be excused.

This perception gives new meaning to accountability, and confronts the manipulator with his or her shadowy motives. Western history would be very different had this interpretation prevailed. An interpretation, by the way, that is much closer to polytheism than it is to proclaimed monotheism. I say proclaimed monotheisms because all the major ones, Judaism, Christianity, and Islam have splintered many times over the centuries.

Evidence for the Moral Law can be found in other highly evolved mammals such as the Bonobo chimpanzee as well as the dolphin. Biologists, neural scientists like Damasio, and animal psychologists demonstrate the emergence of consciousness and self in animals that express moral behavior, either toward members of their own species, or even generalize moral behavior across species. It is demonstrated, therefore, that laws of evolution contain emergent algorithms that express themselves as we move up the Tree of Life itself. Projecting this awareness, I postulate that life forms across the universe will follow similar laws. We must also come to acknowledge these laws as we set out to explore beyond our solar system. Continuing conflict with our own nature is not compatible with the laws of science, which appear to be expressed universally throughout the cosmos.

153

Glen A. Just

The self strives for integration and unity as a life force, and this striving naturally brings sentient beings and animals with consciousness and a self to ever larger realms of identification: from family to tribe, from tribe to nation, from nation to universe. Unity, wholeness, and integration of functional capacities, whether they are in the body proper, brain, or the brain's emergent mind, eventually leads to identification with all planetary as well as extra-planetary life forms. It is not possible to experience the beauty of one's inner self and not have this identification. Conversely, when the beauty of self, the beauty within our DNA's potential, and the beauty of all forms and structures throughout the universe is accredited to one unknowable, all powerful entity who exists in the form of a tribal elder, we become paupers in the shadow of riches. I did not create the beauty of my mind, consciousness, or ability to reason, but I surely admire it. There is no conflict here between the theist and the atheist.

DEMISE OF POLYTHEISM AND MONOTHEISM

Shamanic experiences, once we learn to control and direct them, lose their mystic quality. What we get in their place is an enlarged sense of our own responsibility to self, others, and nature. Shamanic experiences place polytheism and monotheism on equal footing, because both originate in the human psych as abstractions. Both enjoy similar and overlapping mental capacities, and both are led by individuals who currently and throughout history have claimed that these capacities are God or Spirit given, and therefore, claiming to be emissaries from the Beyond.

Neural science recognizes the Self (Soul) as an emergent from the biological capacity contained within our own brains. Neural philosophy builds the blocks from which thought and reasoning is derived. Together, disembodied reasoning of Aristotle, Saint Augustine, Descartes, Kant, and others is set aside as interesting history, but not something that explains our current understanding of mind, consciousness, evolution, or biology.

The areas of expertise claimed by religion in terms of human nature, origin of the Moral Law, and extra-body constructed concepts such as spirits and angels are all being systematically eliminated. We are left with our very human, unadulterated religious natures as the shrouds of dogma drop away. The last vestige of traditional monotheistic religion's historical claim to explain the human soul has slipped to the edge of the precipice, and is about to fall over it as we come to know consciousness, self, and our embodied religious nature. This is not the death, but the founding of spirit.

It becomes ever clearer that traditional religion and its dogmas have historically been able to slow and delay this progression, however, the forces of the human mind, whether designed by God or nature, push the clouds of darkness back into the night, and let the rays of nature's and God's sunshine through.

I have been impressed with Genghis Kahn's view of God and religion for many years, and not just because he gave religious freedom to the largest empire in history. He saw the Great Blue Sky as sheltering all humanity. Under this canopy existed many religions, and his was also different from those of his conquered territories, but they were all equal in his eyes. The Great Kahn recognized the universal religious nature in all of us, and thought it natural that we should express this nature in our own ways. Religious freedom meant respect for God as well as respect for our own innate being. For the Great Kahn, God spoke to us in many different ways, languages, rituals and sensitivities, but we all heard the same voice. Not bad for someone who never went to school! How many centuries it has taken for his philosophy to take root, but there are still many in our world that will kill to deny us this right.

Glen A. Just

ATHEIST FALLACIES

Number 1: Confrontation is used by Dawkins like a battering ram in *The God Delusion,* and he does this with great intelligence and force of argument. Psychologically, his efforts beat upon deaf ears, and his voice is lost in the wind of religious passion and succor that comes from faith, dogmatic faith, or reasoned faith. Basic psychology teaches us that confrontation that is as direct as a Dawkin's arrow wounds deeply, and the wound gets the attention, not the argument. He drives his opponents ever deeper into their belief systems, therefore, he does not lift them to new heights of consideration. I find his mind and arguments interesting, but must fault his limited psychology.

Number 2: **Social and religious movements are not based on reason;** they are based on total consciousness. If they were, we would not have experienced 50,000 to 100,000 years of human existence before modern man learned to walk to the mountain of science. Science is still struggling to free the human spirit from the grip of traditional philosophy and religion. Science is just now shedding the mantle of obscure consciousness and the unknown self. Mutual understanding between science and religion is just now coming onto the horizon. The force of logic of giants like Aristotle and Socrates is now the wisdom of a grade school child. The force of science-based logic that confronts religions, religions that ignore human psychology and neural science, is an energetic force that blows with increasing fury to destroy the straw huts of bodiless reason. Personally, I prefer the gentle summer breeze to a sand storm, but let the storm be, if it is required to sweep away the wreckage, and permit us to make the desert bloom. I strongly believe that I must be sensitive to my fellow creature's religious nature, because we have always demanded expression of this nature. Further, I cannot understand myself by denying my own nature. The fallacies of sociologists and anthropologists who attempt to explain religion purely as a socio-cultural artifact is reflective of Cartesian and Kantian thought.

156

Number 3: Religion is a cultural invention not related to human nature. We are rapidly discarding social models that lack scientific support as we have in psychology and the neural sciences. The standard model of sociology that presented humans as being born *sui generis,* and *tabula rasa,* and were therefore subject to any culturally invented system imaginable, has been made obsolete by psychology and the neural sciences, not by the rhetoric of religion. We can no longer support this simple logic with models of punishment for criminals that are common in the United States. We can no longer support concepts of babies born with blank slates upon which any cultural item can be written, as basic metaphors behind reason and self become increasingly understood and appreciated. We can no longer argue that consciousness is beyond knowing. We can no longer argue that self is an elusive thing beyond concrete understanding. We can no longer argue, I believe, that our religious nature, as taught by false prophets, has an existence outside of our own psyches or DNA expressed algorithms. Religion is coming under the microscope of science, and old ways of thinking are rapidly sliding like sand through the fingers of "ancient" philosophers and dogmatists.

Number 4: Reify means to take something abstract and treat it as though it were a concrete entity or thing. Atheists are treating religion and spirituality as an abstraction created by cultists, large and small, or as cultural creations (fictions) without a base in the "natural" world. A comparable argument might go like this: humans are omnivorous, thus, they can exist on any combination of animal and plant foods. It is all relative in terms of subsistence. So far, so good, but I am quick to add, omnivorous or not, we must pay attention to basic nutrition, and that includes a diet balanced with carbohydrates, protein, minerals, vitamins, and other essentials necessary to maximize our health. We cannot, in other words, ignore dietary needs built into our DNA; not without peril, that is. In like fashion, ignoring our religious nature, assuming it is a totally relative expression of culture, something unrelated to our basic natures, leaves us in a

Glen A. Just

comparative state of extolling our special belief system to the exclusion of our opposing hawkers of philosophies – a strange position for any scientist to be in.

Number 5: The Atheist's product manipulation. Selective arguments of the salesman and manipulator of media emphasizes selling his products good qualities while ignoring the bad, or, even hyping implied attributes that do not exist. The atheist's product manipulation focuses on all the evil that has come from religion, and I do not question that this evil has been monumental. However, the product has also provided purpose, meaning, direction, companionship, love, and community to billions. These are the qualities that have become dominant in the modern world. Is it any wonder that atheism has had an uphill struggle that only the most ferocious warriors are willing to pursue? Atheists are trying to sell the logic of disembodied reasoning to people who feel passion, emotion, and love for each other. It will never happen. The scientific spirit says I must consider all the variables that are interacting in my study, and the missing variable is found in our DNA, the origin of our self, or souls, if you prefer. It exists in an innate religious nature that normal people feel and know through an inner voice called intuition. This intuition being the 95 percent of processing that goes on in our Cognitive Unconscious, to use the words of neural philosophy.

Number 6: Dawkins, paraphrased: If you accept evolution, you must reject religion. This is similar to saying that if you accept religion you must reject sex, or if you accept the idea of good health, you can never eat chocolate. I've stated it simply, but overstatement makes the case. Under what assumptions is Dawkins logic presented? If my contention is correct that by nature we are religious beings, then accepting evolution is to acknowledge our religious nature. Dawkins is not privileged to interpret evolution as though it carried codes in our basic DNA that exclude algorithms such as our religious nature. This position awaits scientific exploration, and explanation through rejection or confirmation. The argument can no more be decided by reasoning than the ancient, and now rather silly,

158

question of how many angels God can put on the end of a pin, if He is all powerful. Obviously, the answer is, at least as many as he put in the Big Bang.

Does Dawkins reject moral law because it is supported by major historical worldviews? Does Dawkins reject moral law because it is supported by major and minor religions, and therefore represents cultural fiction? Does Dawkins reject neural science because it derives consciousness and self from the emergence of mind from brain, which itself emerges from DNA, which itself comes from the fine tuned equations of the physical universe because the linkages are not fully established? There is no law of everything. His argument will hold when the law of everything is derived, and Dawkins is found to be at its center. Until then, let us explore the questions that must be asked of science, rather than simply state that the case is closed.

Number 7: Atheists like Dawkins assume that religion is beyond scientific inquiry and basically support the traditional standard model of sociology and anthropology. Religion is merely a cultural artifact. I am contending that this position is deleterious to understanding human nature. It supports religious dogma by setting up an either or confrontation. It attempts to separate individuals from their religious nature, and this attempt is counterproductive, because it psychologically drives True Believers deeper into their own respective religious dogmas.

Dogma comes into being to codify and simplify religious movements. It helps create a meaningful social organization around which people can rally, share, and develop community. There is nothing negative about this until the dogmatist chooses to, and has power to, exclude open inquiry through power, or the indoctrination of children through exclusiveness in the name of monotheism or polytheism. In the modern world, we come to understand how we can create healthy individuals, healthy families, healthy communities, and healthy nations, and this creation starts with the child in diapers. This understanding does not start with the logic derived only in the setting of one's private library within the university.

Glen A. Just

RELIGIOUS CONCILIENCE

Today's proponents of atheism hammer away at all religions in an attempt to grind them into the dust of history, and ignore related findings from the neural sciences. Treating religions on their own ground, assuming that all religion and its derivations from spirit are cultural creations, just prolongs the argument. Atheists are bound by the same rules of science as are all participants.

Traditional religions hold their dogmas ever tighter as radical movements that thrash wildly in the grip of panic. Self definitions of superiority cannot be maintained dogmatically. Superior positions can only be demonstrated through honest and thorough explorations of self, and our universe through, and understanding of, human nature and science.

My prophet is superior to your prophet has always been decided by the sword, as students of religious movements are vividly aware. Each world religion has its special appeal, such as resurrection of the body, which goes back to at least Egyptian mummification. Likewise, every word of my "bible" is true and given by God, therefore, no one can question it. We have millions of followers, so we cannot be false. Our religion is older than yours, and goes all the way back to Moses. My religion is newer and based on God's latest revelation. Hence, multiple forms of circular reasoning seem never to end.

Religious convergence is not possible when dominance is seen as being achieved through death and destruction, which is justified here on earth when fanatics believe that their future is in Heaven.

Each of these positions crumbles as bedfellows with the view that Earth is the center of the universe, when the telescope of science peers deeply into our souls. And it is now peering deeply into our souls as DNA is unlocked, as animal studies reveal consciousness and all the behaviors of an aware self in other species, as neural science comes to explain the inner workings of our minds, as astral travel, reincarnation, speaking-in-tongues, automatic writing, and other mystic states come under our control and direction.

The mind of the dogmatist is being overwhelmed by science. Increasing numbers of world peoples are recognizing the contradictions of traditional religions, discovering their own religion's history, and generally responding in one of two ways: anger, or finding a meaningful substitution through which their innate religious nature can be expressed. In DNA and in our embodied religious nature, all humankind finds equality.

I predict that the convergence of the trends I have outlined here will relegate all traditional religions, monotheism, polytheism, and atheism, to history. And recognition of and respect for our own evolutionarily derived natures will emerge to create the first world order based on respect, love, and harmony between all peoples. Indeed, this may be the only future we have.

11 - SCIENCE AND THEOLOGY RECONCILED

ELIMINATING CONFLICT

I have used three of Damasio's books as references because I find his researched-based thoughts and speculations to resonate with my altered reality experiences. His enjoyment of and appreciation for Spinoza's thoughts and life exceeds my own. Over 50 years ago when I first read Spinoza, I found him to be one of the few rational thinkers about God and spirituality in Western thought up to the 1960s. Spinoza felt like a big brother to me, and I don't mean as in George Orwell's *1984*. Being in altered states of reality takes one to the bedrock of emotions and feelings, and we experience a clarity that is missing from our normal cluttered cognitive processes. I often thought that if Spinoza did not actually enter similar altered states, he approached the edge of these experiences enough to intuit them. I have not changed my mind about him to date, but I do now experience Spinoza as being less of a mystic than I did at that time.

Damasio's analysis of how consciousness develops in its extended human forms, and how the self and autobiographical self accompany this development to make us the complex thinking creatures that we are, permits analysis of human ethics, morality, and the emergence of complex social systems. He moves across a landscape familiar to neural scientists and the bio-social sciences to a territory more familiar to social scientists and philosophers. I believe that it is impossible to think about our own spirituality, mystic experiences, or even what life means without a framework compatible with this scope and vision. Historical sages from Aristotle to Saint Augustine to Spinoza and modern versions of utopias engage in this speculation. It is a natural progression. What is needed as science comes to fill in the gaps as we move from particle physics to DNA to social structure, is explanation of the causative dynamics as each level is articulated with the next.

Religions are feeling based social institutions, and Damasio's explanatory model of emotion, feeling, consciousness, and self supports my experiences of altered states of consciousness. In turn, ASC support perceptions that something outside of one's body and brain is at work. They form the basis for spirits, angels, devils, gods, and God as realities external to us; they form the framework of an external soul; they form the ethereal substance from which all supernatural objects are created. These infrequent but common shamanic experiences objectify lesser concrete experiences of normal individuals, as they experience awe and wonder of the "magical" world in which we have historically lived.

Once we identify these processes of creation within ourselves, the mystery of primitive mindsets disappears. God and the Moral Law are once again placed in their natural abode, and tension between the theist and atheist is reduced. The ultimate question remaining is the placement of God within a random act of cosmic evolution and the formation of life that results, or in a process that is set in motion by an Intelligent Universe.

Damasio sees feelings as necessary states for the appearance of ethical behavior in the course of human evolution; I can't agree with him more. Specifically, in *Looking for Spinoza,* he says: "In brief, whether one sees ethical principles as mostly nature-based or religious-based development, it appears that the compromise of emotion and feeling early in human development would not have boded well for the emergence of ethical behavior." (158) I will not duplicate his argument, but

163

the essence is this: consciousness and the emergence of self permits empathy and identification with our own kind, which in turn leads to awareness that what we want others to do to us we must first do to them. In effect, he identifies the source of the Moral Law as I have subjectively come to know it. Damasio's progression from proto-consciousness and self to eventually lay the base for social ethics is a plausible model for evolutionary biology, as well as providing a model for individual development; approximately, ontogeny recapitulates phylogeny.

There is no conflict between science and religion here. A natural explanation based on human biology leads to the Moral Law without recourse to various super-magical explanations. Conflict is eliminated when we see the mechanism for Moral Law to be programmed within our own brains and minds.

Spinoza's concept of the God within us offers a compatible understanding from which Damasio draws substance. In the 1950's when I first enjoyed Spinoza, my reaction was similar. Later, through reflection of my own mystic states, I came to realize why. A God within is just as abstract as a God out there, but very concrete at the same time. Spinoza is mystical only if one denies their own flesh and blood existence, and instead, substitutes spirits and entities independent of this flesh and blood. As a person with shamanic realities, this was not possible for me. In altered states I feel the unity and wholeness of being identified with the "other" or others. Ultimately, altered states lead one to identify with all life, nature, and the mysteries beyond them.

I believe one approximates this feeling of wholeness as they reach higher levels of maturity and integrated brain function, or are able to construct cognitive explanations for themselves and the world around them that they then accept as being comprehensive. When these comprehensive worldviews are created, there is a dynamic feedback loop to the emotions, and one prepares to move to the next level. Spinoza fits this model as he thinks deeply about God, religion, self, and utopian conditions to bring it all together. I don't know if he ever had altered reality experiences, because his private life was so private. However, I have no doubt that he could have arrived at similar understandings cognitively, especially when his reasoning was so well balanced on a stable plateau of emotion and feelings, and the brain states that occur from this balance. His lifestyle surely met these requirements, and for me, explains why he maintained such an uncomplicated, unpretentious, and simple existence. A little reflection about simple life styles leads one to a similar conclusion: the monk, the person of Kant, or Spinoza rarely venturing about geographically, or other great figures in history, whose simple surroundings permitted an uncluttered view of the world. This environment is conducive to cognitive clarity that is dependent upon emotional purity.

Traditional religions create conflict and tension for those of us who find logical contradictions in their history, personalities, assumptions, and misuse of science and logic. These contradictions have naturally been challenged throughout history, but most significantly during the Enlightenment, when the church still possessed the power to kill, and used it extensively, and the next most lethal weapon of organized religion, which is the fear of hell fire and damnation, the eternal burning, and torture in hell. If an American parent tortured their children with such rhetoric, they would be hauled into court.

As leading social institutions that can help stabilize social order and provide meaning to its followers, religious orders have an obligation to modernize their dogmas. This process of modernization becomes impossible with a model that denies the findings of science and historians. The challenge for traditionalists is this: Why do you continue to deny the possibility that God can act through Its own laws? (I purposefully do not give God a gender identity as I can't imagine a Being that is all powerful, all knowing, and who moves effortlessly through time having my body configuration.) For the naturalist, and here I exclude the atheist's model that is based on an understanding of natural law that is incomplete, as I think we have a long way to go before humanity has such knowledge, there is no conflict finding these forces in our biology.

Damasio says: "I must confess I do not favor the attempts to neurologize religious experiences, especially when the attempts take the form of identifying a brain center for God, or justifying God and religion by finding correlates in brain scans."

165

(Spinoza: 284) I completely agree with his comments about finding God in a specific brain center, or through machine scans. However, finding God in algorithms of DNA is not on the same level of simplicity, but rather, the next level or two of abstraction. The algorithms in our DNA are expressed in our ability to identify with others in acts such as empathy, and the realization that what we do to others can be, and probably will be, done to us. The Hand of God is not a preacher banging a Bible on his or her lectern, or a Jihadist blowing his fellow world citizens into eternity.

Damasio says that autobiographical memory creates "goodness" and "badness." The forces of darkness and lightness in ageless metaphor spring from this conception. Goodness and badness comes into being because of our awareness that acts of well being for self are dependent upon reciprocity of others. I may be overusing Damasio's words; however, he clearly addresses the biological roots of morality and social ethics. It is interesting that we can start at so many different points and all reach the city of morality at the same time: Neural science of consciousness leads to social ethics. Spinoza's conception of God within, and our biological self, leads to the moral person and the moral state; Aristotle's conception of the most finite unit of matter, to consciousness, to the good state, follows a similar progression. It is inevitable that deep reasoning moves across this landscape. Let us now contemplate 2084, not 1984.

MORAL LAW AND SOCIAL ORDER

There is not a direct causative relationship between our neurobiological makeup and ethical behavior. I never intended to imply such a direct relationship when I talked about DNA emergents and algorithms. E.O. Wilson looks at this relationship in his attempts to reconcile biology and emergent social patterns in society. There is considerable work left before we can walk through the causative chain from neuron pathways to social order, but the convergence of knowledge from multiple disciplines, I believe, will inevitably take us there. Nevertheless, altered states and their interpretations can facilitate this coming together of knowledge fronts. And I believe it is a much overlooked scientific enterprise; one that should have been addressed in the 1600's when Spinoza made such a valiant attempt.

I appreciate Damasio's fondness for Spinoza, and his recounting of the religious forces that acted on this great thinker. Most significantly, Damasio points out the role of religious suppression that stopped this necessary analysis – a black hole of ignorance that is currently being reversed.

I like Damasio's idea, as he expressed it in *Spinoza,* that society would not develop increasingly sophisticated social structures to support and shape dynamically functional organizations without the growth of autobiographical memory, and the ethics spawned thereby, hence, support for my argument for life forms throughout the universe expressing similar emergent algorithms. Life forms will have to pass through these stages of development or something parallel for them, to reach sophisticated levels of organization on which the accumulation of scientific knowledge becomes possible. I am not concerned about aliens abusing humans; I am concerned with helping humans reach a stage of moral development where it becomes impossible for us to abuse aliens, which means, of course, we are no longer capable of abusing ourselves.

Damasio says in *Spinoza* that, "… feelings may have been a necessary grounding for ethical behaviors long before the time humans even began to deliberate construction of intelligent norms and social conduct." (160) He is generally supporting my argument that we humans are religious by nature, and helps trace this progression by references in animal psychology. This is also a stage of development that the evolutionary biologists must take into consideration.

What we experience in mystic states has less cultural filtering than experiences that rely directly on teachings from our culture and its institutions of organized religion. By this statement, I mean that intra-psychic experiences have greater freedom to create worlds of harmony and unity than institutionalized, dogmatic religion does. Historically, as I see it, these creative mystic experiences have been used at critical times in our social development to explain a complex of forces acting upon ourselves and our group. Subsequently, the explanations are adopted and codified, and some linger on in institutionalized religions. However, with the large scale development of dogmatic monotheisms, this creative process has been blocked. The base for knowledge accumulation is strengthened through socially stable communities, but at the same time, monotheistic constraints create conflict between dogma and science. How can we break through this dilemma?

Damasio talks about groups and individuals who are not ethical, and reflects on humanity's dark side. He points out differences between members of the in-groups and out-groups to which we apply or withhold ethical conduct. The Old Testament is especially good at identifying enemies and striking them dead; the God of vengeance and wrath as it is so frequently portrayed, versus the God of love in the New Testament. Noting the light side and the dark side of humanity does not bring us to clarify of understanding. I don't think we can leave the issue this naked.

My experience as a mystic contends that integrated personalities continue to move to higher levels of neural integration, higher levels of consciousness, and greater degrees of unity and harmony. The dark side is not inevitable. The dark side is an immature level of individual cognitive-emotional development that I believe we can transcend as a species. Utopian models cannot be created without taking human biological, neural, and social integration into consideration, and this vision has science at its core.

Further, we cannot transcend current group levels of ethical behavior until we unravel mystic states, until we bring religion to a level of maturity equal to other areas of scientific development, and until we create a social structure that permits these first two stages of the sacred and secular to be expressed compatibly and with harmony.

This vision of human development sees world harmony coming into being through science marching arm and arm with a compatible religion. The deep inner needs of you and me are not met in an Ivory Tower of "pure" Kantian thought. Our total self of thought and feeling must be acknowledged, made safe, and cherished, if we wish to progress as a species. Contemporary monotheisms, which stress traditional dogma, are not yet capable of reaching this plateau.

In *Looking for Spinoza:* "... the beneficial role of the culture depends, in large measure, on the accuracy of the scientific picture of human behavior the culture uses to forge its future path." (164) Religion is at a crossroad in world history, and I contend has an obligation to evolve compatibility with science, thereby helping world people move to a higher level of integration and harmony. The Chinese government's emphasis on building a harmonious society, and a harmonious world in the 21st Century, reflects this vision, and it is reflected even more clearly with its emphasis on Chinese characteristics. There is an explicit as well as implicit assumption that something has gone wrong with the Western model, and China must exercise caution as it creates a new beginning. This cautious approach to and partial rejection of Western thought and culture is inevitable, given the West's inability to reconcile religion with a stable social order. Radical expressions of monotheisms, and I do mean monotheisms, are still generating widespread destruction in the Muslim, Judaic, and Christian worlds as we progress into the 21st Century.

The study of social emotions is in its infancy says Damasio, and I especially agree when we consider the role of unexamined states of altered consciousness and the role they play in monotheisms. Damasio says in Spinoza that "... if the cognitive and neurobiological investigations of emotions and feelings can join forces with, for example, anthropology and evolutionary psychology, it is likely that some of the suggestions in this chapter can be tested." (169)

Damasio reaches from neurons to norms in this statement. However, I believe we must be careful not to base this marriage on untested social theory that remains rampant into the 21st Century. Each stage of integration must be thoroughly tested, and I can't imagine this happening without complex, dynamic models based on complexity theory and models supporting emergent social structure that are based on related and substantiated theories. Contemporary sociology leaves much to be desired in this respect, as I have earlier noted in the example of sociological criminology.

It is unfortunate that Gnostic literature was destroyed so extensively by the Catholic Church after codification of dogma following the Council of Nicaea in 325 CE. My mystic experiences, altered reality episodes, resonate with Gnostic "feelings" that God resides in each one of us, and it is within ourselves that we come to know Him. My understanding and interpretations differ, but the experiences of shared altered realities have much in common with Gnostic writings. If you are Christian, I believe that early destruction of these works was unfortunate. This destruction denied us the Gnostic Jesus.

First-hand accounts of these experiences, as I have discussed them in *Autobiography of a Ghost,* can provide insight into our mind's functioning, and provide a broad picture of the neural processes being expressed, the neural pathways employed, and the varied expressions of different brain centers in creating these intra-psychic experiences. And, in doing so, we significantly increase our understanding of self, soul, and religion.

SOC IAL ORDER AND THE MYSTIC

Mind of the Mystic contends that humans are religious by nature; that converging trends across the sciences, especially neural science, neural philosophy, developmental psychology, social biology, and emerging scientific studies of religion, support this position. Neural scientists such as Damasio and LeDoux are refining our understanding about the underpinnings of human emotions, feelings, and consciousness, and their work relies heavily on biology. I believe that as we increasingly reveal these mysteries, we will further unlock the underpinnings of our religious nature, which I have referred to as the algorithms in our DNA, and in this process, increasingly clarify how the Moral Law naturally emerges and is expressed individually. As we come more fully to explain altered states of reality from a neural science and developmental psychological perspective, the mystery of the mystics disappears, and the religious dogmas supported by these mystic persons is reinterpreted. Consequently, the edifice of traditional monotheisms cries out for a new integrative paradigm.

Damasio sees religion emerging in human history as an organizational pattern (social structure) to help regulate interpersonal affairs that promote and create social harmony. This view is very main stream. Then he goes on to look at humanity's dark side, and various aspects of inter-group conflict, thereby leaving possible bridging mechanisms unexamined. What we miss is insight that will help us move to the next level of understanding; a level of knowledge integration that comes eventually from an increasingly complex and comprehensive set of interdisciplinary studies. I agree with Damasio that work by individuals like E. O. Wilson is crucial if we are to make this next step. But, this next step cannot be accomplished using the standard models of the social sciences and philosophy. It must come to rely on the newer probabilistic models derived from complexity theory, neural science, biology, and testable hypotheses.

I am also stressing the importance of putting the role of religion in individual lives and the social order in a model that permits humanity to take this next step, and contend that our religious nature is often misrepresented because we fail to understand mystic states. An empirical understanding of altered realities addresses traditional religions, especially monotheisms, and dysfunctional models in philosophy, sociology, and anthropology. The age is upon us, as evidenced by scientists such as Damasio, who dared stick his academic chin out on consciousness studies, for us to take this next step.

I have argued that inter-group conflict cannot be eliminated if world religions continue to guard historical dogma as though it were the teachings of God. Increasingly, the teachings of God are to be found in the vision of Einstein who saw God's hand expressed through the laws of nature. The cracks in monotheistic dogma are too broad and wide for these edifices to stand. The discomfort that comes from ignoring science, or suppressing scientific knowledge such as evolution, is not sustainable for a growing number of world people. We feel our spiritual nature within, and yearn for communion with this biological nature and each other. This is the nature that makes us social, the nature that makes us devils or angels, and the nature that can take us to peace and harmony, to the stars, or to extinction.

It is time for a new religious paradigm. World religions that ignore our basic human nature, as increasingly revealed by science, have become a roadblock to social evolution and world peace. Contemporary monotheism and polytheism are obsolete philosophies, small or large, primitive or urbane, and must be brought into resonance with nature's plan. Pastoral monotheism continues to thrive on the poverty and desperation of the world's multiplying billions. Yes, it offers temporary emotional support to millions, but at the same time, it uses dogma to prevent the creation of a functional world order, and it does not permit distribution of world resources or a rational development of population and pollution control to guarantee a future for humanity.

However, let us not just walk away from our religious history as Dawkins does. Let us acknowledge the important role it has played in helping to bring us to a new plateau of understanding through science. Looking across the merging landscape of history and science, we should appreciate our struggle to know our world, our self, and our universe. The dynamic interplay between science and religion is not finished, and I don't believe it can be called to an end with non-religious dogmatic pronouncements. But this dynamic interplay of science and religion cannot take the next step to enlightenment by using two thousand year old dogmas based on magical thinking and pastoral insights.

World leaders, such as President G. W. Bush, have used archaic thinking to promote their individual conceptions of God, and in doing so, have brought much of the world to its knees. Fortunately, weapons of mass destruction were not part of these ignoble steps and misuse of human resources. I propose that a world leadership that will eventually triumph in terms of sustainable civilizations will be one that successfully integrates science and humanity's religious nature, not those who insist on archaic dogma, or deny our religious nature.

WHY MYSTICISM?

I believe that scientific analysis and understanding of mystic states has been neglected to such an extent that it is one of the major roadblocks preventing civilization from moving to the next higher plane of development. Failure to explore our religious natures scientifically has left interpretation of our religious natures to the ancients and those who cloak themselves in the same animal skins. I have proposed that it is necessary to study the God within through exploration of altered reality states, because these techniques permit us to look at the phenomena from the inside-out. Psychoanalysis and scientific methodologies have not yet adequately revealed how we experience altered states. Scientific methodologies explain the brain center's operations and mental functions, but they do not provide a complete picture of altered consciousness, which I am contending is a crucial part of knowledge integration necessary to fully address the relationship between religion and science. Leaving the final explanation of altered realities to the priest or guru is a mistake. It is similar to asking a long-term criminal to explain his behavior, and then believing his every word.

Failure to move the study of religion along scientific lines has created great tension in our social fabric and world cultures. We continue to practice group murder which we euphemistically call war. We continue to see the underclass and the poor as inevitable parts of social life, and justify this misuse of our fellow humans by reference to the Bible. We continue to destroy damaged young people in socially sanctioned dens of abuse that we call prison. We continue, we continue. Not only is the unexamined life not worth living, but the unexamined self, the self confined to dogma, consciousness diminished – all un-examined – speak ill for humanity's future.

Knowledge integration that leads to world harmony and social peace requires that we bring together inter-disciplinary studies from the neural sciences, developmental psychology,

173

evolutionary biology, historical religions, and philosophies. It necessitates bringing all fields of inquiry onto a plane of comparable scientific inquiry with supporting methodologies. This includes the formal study of mysticism and altered states with scientific methods used to analyze world theisms.

Lastly, I am contending that world religions that pay attention to human nature, biology, and science, will become stronger, not superfluous. The fast pace of new knowledge accumulation, combined with an increasingly fragmented social order, begs us to find better ways to support the religious nature within each of us. We are possessors of the Moral Law, a law that increasingly appears inherent in the algorithms of our DNA. We can come to experience ever greater joy, peace, harmony, and interpersonal fulfillment when we are able to unite science and religion.

Evolution denied is equivalent to denying our own nature, but worst of all, it denies discovery of the God within. Failure to look into this last cave of human consciousness has cost humanity dearly. Science has not been the cave's denying gatekeeper, but monotheistic religions have been. Add dogmatic atheism that helps block spiritual understanding, and we have a deadly combination. Let us agree to correct this error of history, and in doing so, thank Spinoza for being one of the first clear thinkers to set us straight.

MULTIPLICITY

Light, in its ultimate sense of being
knows that it is time itself
Space nurtures light
that slow moving creature of time,
and God smiles.

Theologians define Logos,
forever the logic of One
Science smiles at Logos
knowing that science is truth itself,

and God laughs.

My eyes are your sight,
your sight is my knowing.
My mind has your thoughts,
your thoughts are my being,
And God rejoices.

12 - INSIGHTS

Insight 1: Altered reality intra-psychic experiences occur when neural structures are combined in new configurations and process synaptic exchanges in unusual ways. As I discuss my own experiences in **Autobiography of a Ghost**, creating new neural configurations leads us to speak in tongues, experience astral travel, ghosts and angels, reincarnation, automatic writing, and spirit possession. Individuals throughout history and across the modern world have these experiences, but they are unusual enough that those who do not experience them come to believe that those of us who do are in contact with God or the supernatural. Most of us, at least initially, come to believe traditional explanations for our own altered reality experiences, and some continue to be True Believers throughout their lifetimes. We come to accept explanations for our ASC experiences given to us by our own cultures and religions, and we become mystics, prophets, or shamans. However, if the experiences disagree with our culture's traditional worldviews or religious philosophies, or are too extreme, we are labeled misfits, agents of the devil, or a multitude of other uncomplimentary names.

As we come to understand the origin of ASC experiences, it becomes obvious that neural configurations that process input from our senses in culturally normative ways are suspended when new or different configurations emerge and create these

175

true-to-life altered realities. New configurations can emerge due to trauma, which was my own experience, or any extremely stressful condition such as dehydration, starvation, life threatening episodes, or unusual physical changes due to tumors, cancer, war, or drugs. In my history, smothering attacks by my mother, which led to my death experience when I was two years old, along with extreme neglect, brought about my first out-of-body experience, visitation by angels, the appearance of my Guardian Angel, and endless visitation by a haunting ghost. These intra-psychic experiences were just as real to me at the time as eating lunch.

Native Americans vision quests were and are achieved through fasting, exposure to the physical elements, use of drugs such as peyote, traumatic events such as war, or the Sun Dance. Related altered reality experiences by various people from around the world, as revealed through historical sources such as the Bible, and numerous ethnographies by anthropologists, are well known. Typically, supernatural contact was assumed, and the shamanic experience was interpreted as putting one in contact with whatever spirit or spirits the culture assumed was out there. When the shaman's experience, the mind of the mystic, becomes part of a major religious movement, it is assumed that the visions or messages come directly from that group's God, or gods, or spirit world.

Insight 2: Visions and altered reality states are culturally dependent and come from our own minds or psyches. Understanding our basic human capacities for these religious experiences forces us to confront their varied explanations historically and world-wide. This mystic capacity is not only universal, but stems from altered neural configurations in our own brains; configurations that emerge as mine did from my own psyche.

ASC is expressed in similar fashions across cultures as it is part of how our minds are created and maintained. Awareness of this emergent capacity across our species is demonstrated by the universality of similar religious experiences throughout history and across cultures. Most telling, however, we are now able to document the origin of these intra-psychic experiences when we create and control them experientially. Further, it is not the variety of interpretations for intra-psychic experiences that is critical, it is the basic human capacity that makes these experiences inevitable that demands explanation. I find interpretations of various experiences of altered realities in pre-literate as well as modern cultures interesting because they parallel my own. Therefore, I am forced to recognize that experiences of altered reality, experiences that form the basis of both polytheistic and monotheistic religions, are naturally determined by the structure of our brains, and how our minds develop from this structure.

Changes in neural patterning, which are sensitive to multiple triggers, can bring about new configurations induced by anxiety, depression, physical trauma, or unusual physical changes in our brains caused by blood clots, tumors, and cancer. It is now common knowledge that chemical levels within the brain change under extreme conditions, as do operating neural configurations.

Brain plasticity permits compensation when one part of the brain is damaged or common neural pathways are altered. At a different level, or more specifically, in new configurations, brain plasticity using new neuronal combinations produces altered states of reality and mystic experiences. This is the crux of my experience and argument.

Lazy brains, especially for the elderly, are reconditioned by neural scientists like Michael Merzenich at the University of California, San Francisco. This reconditioning increases memory and probably grows a limited number of new brain cells. In my case, I simply reconditioned my own brain as a university student, and continued this process throughout most of my adult years. In 1958 I was unaware of how I was modifying inter-neuronal connections. I just kept creating new effects that I found interesting and wanted to explore further.

I thought brain restructuring, with a focus on learning, was possible from the courses I was taking in psychology, and the information I was discovering in world literature related to religion and social thought. It seemed obvious to me at that time that my brain was also producing new cells; however, this contemporary fact was not accepted by the medical community in the 1950's. And the type of self experiments I was conducting were outside the scope of popular analyses in the overlapping study areas I was bringing together psychology, hypnosis, mental health profiling through the MMPI, religious studies, the social sciences, philosophy, and a strong dose of experiential experiments.

As a university undergraduate, I thought of reconditioning my brain as a process of rechanneling basic drives. Only later did I come to think of this process as creating new neural configurations. In contrast to the work being done by Merzenich, I didn't use computer programs or hardware as this technology did not exist. I used self-hypnosis to direct expressions within neural pathways that I wanted to reconfigure, e.g., pain control, improved concentration, anxiety reduction, and control over depression. In today's language, I was modifying inter-neuronal connections and pathways.

Insight 3: If newly emerged neural patterns create an external reality moment-to-moment, a reality that family and other observers do not experience, but involve everyday events, the person may be considered psychotic or mentally ill, similar to the interpretation of my MMPI Profile when I was an undergraduate. The Minnesota Multiphasic Personality Inventory did not accommodate those of us with shamanic backgrounds. We simply fell into the critical ranges of psychoses or other related dysfunctions. And in my case, I fit an abnormal MMPI profile in three different critical areas.

To give another example, one of my relatives was in an auto accident and began to have hallucinations a few months later. In one hallucination, he was leaving church with his mother and remarked that his deceased grandfather was walking toward him across the parking lot. Later evaluation determined that a blood clot had formed in his brain as the result of this accident and was the source of his hallucinations. For a number of years he was treated as a psychotic rather than a patient with a life-threatening blood clot in his brain who was hallucinating.

Glen A. Just

Failure to understand altered states of reality and altered neural pathways almost cost this young man his life. Before receiving adequate diagnosis and proper medical intervention, he was inappropriately treated for years by medical personal who assumed that his symptoms were caused by something other than a blood clot. Fortunately, neural science is beginning to take us beyond this darker region of medical practice.

Insight 4: The brain can act as if it were a movie camera. I do not mean that we just use our eyesight to simply scan the world and record**. The brain scans its own recorded landscape, which includes everything external to us as well as everything internal to our psyches.** All of this landscape of the mind, some of which is created whole, is used to produce movies (visions) in the mind, and can be configured in any combination, which is also the case when we dream. If the movie, or movie segment, is experienced during waking hours of normal activity, as was my case as a child and young adult, the episode is considered to be psychotic, and the person is diagnosed as being mentally ill, even though they have normal functions in all other behavioral and perceptual areas.

We call these people psychotic rather than just saying that their inter-neuronal connections are being expressed abnormally. However, in the case of my relative, his blood clot was diagnosed later and additional procedures were implemented to help it dissolve. Gradual shrinking of the clot permitted normal neural processing to reoccur, and that had not returned with antipsychotic drugs. This young man lost critical years of his youth due to inappropriate diagnosis and treatment, and is fortunate to still be alive.

Dream programming is a good example of our brain's capacity to provide us with nighttime movies as we sleep. Physical smothering attacks by my mother when I was still crib confined, as well as later sexual abuse, each created traumatizing nightmares. When I entered the University of Minnesota as an undergraduate, I was plagued by these nightmares but brought them under control with dream programming. I learned to substitute my own programmed

180

dreams for nightmares, and taught my psyche to switch from nightmare to preferred dream whenever the nightmares emerged during sleep. This switching process occurred while I was still asleep, and I did not need to awaken to reactivate the dream program. I was simply using my archive of stored sights and sensations to create real-to-life, pleasing, and sometimes sensuous night movies. I taught my brain this process, and used dream programming to control nightmares into my mid-fifties, when I decided consciously to stop the habit and more fully experience a normal world.

The capacity to automatically control dreams and redirect them while I'm still sleeping stays with me as I age, however, I do not pre-program dreams any longer. Dream programming offered me relief from nightmares, but I also found after weeks of viewing a specific dream-movie that I grew tired of the content. Within a few weeks of teaching myself this ability, I learned to alter the movie scripts. I created alternatives similar to movies recorded on a CD where one can change the endings or sequences through various options that are provided. I changed the dream-movies on demand, adding new segments, deleting movie sequences that became tiresome, or substituting a character with whom I had become bored with one that was new and more exciting.

Eventually I came to realize that this same capacity can be activated by a skilled guru, hypnotist, shaman, or mental health worker to create experiences of astral travel, reincarnation, or false memory. In effect, the dream programming technique can be used to create implanted "objects" that take the place of those that are part of the individual's external experience. In my dreams, the internally created implanted "objects" were treated by my mind as being on an equal par with those from external realities. This process gives insight into cult behavior as the susceptible are brought into the fold.

Insight 5: Reincarnation, Heaven or Hell and everything in between can be experienced through the recombination of different neural networks in our brains. I recounted earlier in **Ghost** of an attempt by an Asian Indian to take me back to a

Glen A. Just

former life as a Plains Indian Chief. I refused his offer, as I assumed he would use a method similar to my own techniques, but the point I'm making is that many individuals believe they are revisiting their former lives because the experiences are completely real. I suspect that some of the gurus leading people through their former lives are also True Believers. Not true in my case, as the gurus' behavior made it very clear that he was searching for a new source of income and had used information from my friends to prepare for my visit.

Insight 6: Visions (dream-movies) are just as real as any other experience that the brain encounters as it involves related changes in brain chemistry, and activation of any of our senses, and draws upon whatever the brain has recorded from external experiences as well as what it has created whole from a myriad of internal sensory re-combinations. As most comprehensive beginning psychology texts demonstrate, we never experience the external world raw and in the buff. We always experience the external world in terms of our sensory processing. Alter the processing, and we alter the reality. A good example being the one hundred million light sensitive cells in our eyes that have external images reduced by a factor of one hundred as they enter the brain. This visual reduction process of our brains is functional and efficient, however, the process by which the brain reconfigures objects it uses in various acts of consciousness permits us to create whatever reality we choose, and the content of this reality can take on a permanent quality.

An interesting awareness that develops from dream programming is the permanent creation of memories from the dreams themselves. I created characters and scenes for my dreams that later appeared on their own in new un-programmed dreams, and were treated in my normal dreams just as factually as events that had occurred in my real life. My mind treated self-created materials as being equally representative of my external world. In my normal dreams, my mind does not make a distinction, but just reaches into its library of stored materials and uses them. This provided me with additional insight into the

182

reality of reincarnation journeys. It helps me understand the True Believer. Further, this appears to be a natural process over which some people lose control when they experience psychosis, and it seems plausible that if we can catch the neural network's memory recording early enough, the process can be consciously redirected by the individual or therapist.

Insight 7: By itself, our brain does not normally become aware of how its own neural networks are operating. The brain is designed to help us make split-second decisions in order to survive, and it does this by preparing automatic responses to events that are harmful to us. For example, you do not think about closing your eyes when something is flying towards them. Instead, you just blink or duck. If you had to think about closing your eyes, they would still be open when the object hit. This design is built into the evolution of our brains as a species, as it is with other mammals that we observe.

Normal to our brains means typical neural processing of the everyday world the brain lives in. When trauma, tumors, neglect, or stress alter these typical neural pathways, the mind may come to treat experiences from newly created neural pathways as coming from outside of itself. We experience mystic phenomena, spirits, the supernatural, God, gods, or whatever explanations have been handed down within our own culture. I am arguing that we must go beyond the pre-scientific interpretation of religious phenomena and embrace the science of how our brains actually work before we can begin to address what is out there in The Intelligent Universe, before we can understand and experience our true religious nature.

The mentally ill are unaware of how their brains are altering normal sensory input, as most of us are unaware of our own Cognitive Unconscious, (as discussed by Lakoff & Johnson) and feel a sense of helplessness and lack of control over these altered states. This loss of control can create panic, anxiety, depression and a sense of helplessness, thereby fostering emotional dependence, degrees of withdrawal from social interaction, even total withdrawal, and a need for pharmaceutical drug intervention to stabilize brain chemistry. In my experience, learning to control altered states of reality returned this control to me, relieved my anxiety and depression, and stabilized my brain chemistry.

Individuals who are having shamanic experiences seek explanations for what is happening to them in a manner similar to the psychotic. They have a need to know. However, those of us with altered reality experiences have a multitude of cultural explanations offered by our favorite religious leader and from our cultures. When our experiences fall within our culture's prevailing religious worldview, we are normal. When our experiences fall outside these worldviews, we are abnormal (psychotic) or possessed by evil spirits or demons.

As I became aware of this process in the 1950's, I found great difficulty discussing related insights with the mental health community. I was either responded to as a lunatic by individuals like the University of Minnesota counselor reading my MMPI Profile, or as a religious mystic. I wasn't comfortable in either camp. Research over the past fifty years generally supports the arguments that I am making. Further, research by professionals like Antonio Damasio and Joseph LeDoux provide depth of insight for the curious reader who is tired of incomplete answers.

Neural science continues to diminish our previous ignorance about ASC. Understanding brain functions from the standpoint of self-control, and redirecting and controlling newly created inter-neuronal connections provides additional insights. Understanding experiences of altered reality as I have discussed them, gives us another window into how our brains operate, as well as explaining our religious nature. It also offers relief from anxiety, nightmares, and depression.

Psychological evaluation in the 1950's did not distinguish-between individuals like me who were aware of creating their own altered reality states, and those who were not. One size fit everyone half a century ago, and we were all evaluated according to the same standards. It was one or two steps up from blood-letting to cure illness, but not yet sufficient to create insight. Even worse, fifty years ago, psychiatry was dominated by Freudian mysticism and psychoanalysis. Rigorously controlled research hasn't been kind to the level of scientific methodology employed during these earlier times. Freud and others are to be applauded for their quest to understand the psyche and breaking with former mental health paradigms, however, their methodology was seriously lacking. But that is the nature of science, as we claw our way to the surface of enlightenment and scientific facts that can be replicated through objective procedures.

Insight 8: Modified inter-neuronal connections and resulting altered states of reality can be brought under individual control through practice by techniques common to various religious practitioners or initiated through hypnosis or self-hypnosis. I discovered this process through self-hypnosis without having contact with traditional shamans, gurus, or prophets, or Freudian-based psychoanalysts. Hence, I was free to look for explanations in the natural sciences. My initial discoveries occurred while I was a university undergraduate in psychology, consequently, I looked for scientific explanations for my own mystic experiences. At the same time, I was seeping myself in religious history, the writings of people like St. Augustine, Thomas Aquinas, Spinoza, Descartes, Kant, western social thought, and a collection of ethnographic studies in anthropology. Gradually, I came to realize that the neural configurations that I was creating produced phenomena similar to what I was discovering in my formal studies, self-directed experiments, and the cultural insights I was gaining from contacts and experiences in the Native American community.

At first I struggled with the idea that there was some kind of Controller in my mind directing these experiences. As an undergraduate, my initial primitive ideas of a mind controller approximated that of a little man sitting in my brain, what some psychology books referred to as a homunculus. When I read Damasio's *Descartes Error* and discovered his analysis of how the self and consciousness comes into being in our minds, I finally had an explanation that was derived from research and the neural sciences. He is very clear that no Little Man sits in my brain and directs my activities, no homunculus, and further outlines a researchable model of consciousness as it emerges from brain and body.

I had been aware that I was teaching my brain to behave in extra-ordinary ways, but I did not have working concepts to express this process in other than religious terms. These terms I found unacceptable, terms that I now know attempt to explain these natural phenomena as coming from outside the brain and mind, from the supernatural. As I gradually learned that I could control and teach my Controller, as I've come to think of this dispersed set of neural functions we call the self, I further realized that I was able to create and direct any ASC, "mystic" neural network pattern that I wanted to experiment with: I left my body at will, I spoke in tongues when I chose to, I enjoyed Zen driving while relaxing, entered the spirit of the bear, or let my psyche mingle with the energy of a thunderstorm or Northern Lights.

Insight 9: Metaphorical constructs that I parsimoniously associate with Lakoff and Johnson's *Philosophy in the Flesh* deepened my understanding of how the brain derives and uses concepts of space, time, size, and other related constructs to represent its relationship with the external world, our own bodies, and our minds. Universally we use these metaphorical constructs to represent both our external and internal worlds. The capacity is universal and constructs are similar across our species if not the same at their most basic level; however, metaphorical constructs become increasingly complex with more sophisticated speech and conceptual development.

Interpretations of our external and internal world gradually emerge as we become social beings, along with different cultural configurations that combine the entire sensations of our individual worlds of experience. Lesson learned: human metaphorical capacity provides a similar base for experiences of altered reality, but images within these mystic experiences take on forms shaped by our own culture and the interpretations we derive from them. Culture does not operate on a blank slate of the mind, but configures content created from our basic metaphorical capacity that then comes to be expressed through the neural structures that are also common across our species.

More specifically, we do not simply create ghosts, spirits, spirit possession, Gods, and gods through an external cultural process. This interpretation of causation must be incorrect as expressed by historical sociologists and anthropologists. We create content representing similar forms such as ghosts and angels from the algorithmic capacity in our DNA. This content is inserted into the conscious and unconscious imaging capacity which develops, consequently, spirit interpretations belong to our cultures as collective human interpretive responses. Therefore, our religiosity is a natural biological emergent. The Cosmic Shaman starts from and ends with human nature, as all common religious experiences do. Both polytheistic and monotheistic interpretations of religious experiences start and stop with our basic biological capacities. They are driven by the same mechanisms of causation.

Insight 10: The Controller (but not homunculus) can be taught to direct functions that are normally automatic (autonomic nervous system functions) and be in charge of them during waking hours or in dream programming. This includes all human senses as we teach our Controller to master, direct, or suppress them, including, Zen driving, astral travel, dream programs, pain reduction or elimination, and other related manipulation of our senses that I have discussed in earlier chapters, and in *Ghost*. Initially, as a university student, I practiced controlling pain by desensitizing various areas of my body. These were areas that I could stick pins into without feeling pain. Also, controlling my heartbeat, breathing, or opening closed sinuses. After I gained this level of control, I went on to create dream programs to conquer my long-term nightmares.

Insight 11: Our minds become integrated as we experience an increasingly stable environment; interactively, a stable environment is experienced as we integrate our psyches

cognitively and emotionally. We know that when we are anxious, others tend to mirror our anxiety and to a similar degree become uncomfortable. We change our interactions with others as we change ourselves. Individuals who cannot control their own anxiety or depression select friends and social situations with whom they are compatible. Cognitive and emotional integration opens up a larger social world with all its possibilities, and at the far end of this path, we come to identify with the whole of humanity, as we come to experience unity and wholeness.

I am contending that the integrated self experiences peace, quietude, wholeness, focus, and total identification with others, including multiple life forms. And the ultimate state of human maturity, which I believe is available to all normal brains, is nonviolent. At this level, we experience the Moral Law as a natural emergent from our minds, brains, and native biology.

I stabilized my brain chemistry by directing my Controller to take charge of the anxiety and depression that I was experiencing. I was suffering from extreme anxiety and considerable depression, and experiencing related complications in my studies and life. But I knew little about brain chemistry in 1958. I simply implanted routines in my mind at the behavioral level to control anxiety and depression. It was some years later that I began to digest literature in the neural sciences. Self-integration also meant that critical elevations on my MMPI began to disappear and return to normal levels. And, by the time I graduated with my bachelor's degree, MMPI test results in paranoid-schizophrenia, obsessive-compulsive, and psychopathic personality areas tested within normal ranges.

Changes in my lifestyle included extending periods of study from twenty minutes to four and then eight hours of continuous concentration with exceptional recall, for example, recall in the 98th percentile with one reading. I was sleeping full nights without nightmares for the first time in my life, and no longer found it necessary to approach sleep through exhaustion. My tendency to become angry at others in irritating situations was almost eliminated. I was intense, as described by my friends, and much of the hyper-vigilance I had learned from my parent's brutality was replaced by focused and appropriate attention to what was happening around me. Most of these changes took place within a year of my newly implemented routines, which I initiated and directed through the use of self-hypnosis.

Insight 12: Integration of our psyches comes in stages, but each stage of higher integration improves self-control and tends to increase our social network. As indicated in insight number 11, mental health not only develops and changes in stages as is commonly understood, but integration of our psyches in terms of eliminating dysfunctions, such as anxiety, is central to our movement from stage to stage. When I implemented various routines to control anxiety, depression and nightmares, I became conscious of being less agitated, anxious, and depressed. I began to sleep better, was less exhausted at bedtime, was gaining a much improved level of concentration, and had an improved sense of being whole. I developed a sense of psychic unity and peace within my soul. Over time, I consciously experienced a sense of wholeness and a new level of intra-psychic integration that I had not previously known.

To continue the metaphor with my Controller, unity, being centered and focused, meant that I was expending less psychic, emotional, and physical energy completing normal daily routines of work and study. Throughout the day, a hyper-vigilant individual wastes a tremendous amount of physical and emotional energy by paying attention to all the fine details occurring in his life, and that was definitely true for me. As my self-therapy was implemented, I no longer had to deal with the energy demands made by anxiety, depression, and hyper-vigilance. I truly became a new person. As I gradually conquered my history of family dysfunction, mystic states and altered realities were finally placed in their appropriate context. I wasn't crazy, and I wasn't Jesus.

Insight 13: Social maturity occurs when cognitive and emotional integration reaches a level that permits harmonious interpersonal contact and life-goal realization; however, it is noted that adult maturity has many additional

189

levels that we can achieve. As a child and young adult who moved on average three times every two years, I was often in situations of physical confrontation, in geography where boys and young men solved interpersonal conflicts physically. As I integrated my mental functions during my first year at the University of Minnesota, I found this physical history distasteful, and vowed to give it up. And, I did. Over the following two to three decades I became increasingly pacifistic as I passed through higher levels of maturity, became less restless, and slowly projected the intra-psychic peace I was experiencing onto the world around me. Gradually, I came to realize that emotional and cognitive integration expresses itself in interpersonal harmony.

Insight 14: Humanity becomes one unit of people at higher levels of self integration and maturity, and we come to personally experience the Moral Code. Continuing from Insight 13, my integrated psyche eventually came to experience all humanity as one family. I believe this personal feeling of being part of one human family is inevitable once we tear down the cultural walls of prejudice and discrimination taught by our respective cultures. However, these cultural walls fall away by themselves as we reach higher levels of self-integration and maturity. This has often been presented, and referred to, as mystic phenomena in various religions and philosophies.

It is at this point of our personal development that the Moral Law of C. S. Lewis comes into being. From this perspective, the Moral Law is in our DNA, but not something that automatically occurs. It requires a stable environment, loving family, and personal opportunities for each one of us to integrate cognitively and emotionally. The Moral Law is unknown to the fragmented or corrupted self. The fragmented self must become integrated before it can experience what is meant by, "do unto others as you would have others do unto you."

Insight 15: Most forms of punishment, especially those of harsh imprisonment, do not permit the individual psyche to

move closer to the moral code that is dependent upon emotional and cognitive integration. Harsh punishment fails due to brutal living conditions that require hyper-vigilance, or the assumption that deprivation alone produces character. It does not. Righteousness is not obtained by just appealing to an external god. Righteousness is obtained through love and nurturing of the soul, and that is not a mystic soul disconnected from our bodies, but a soul that naturally emerges from our biology. It is obtained by acknowledging and supporting how the moral law is expressed though normal, healthy living conditions. We cannot deny what is built into our DNA, nor should we.

The atheist sees morality as occurring naturally without God, whereas the theist sees the source of morality as coming from God. Nevertheless, we are bound by the same human condition when we recognize that the Moral Law comes from within ourselves when it is nurtured properly. It does not occur through direct appeal to an all knowing Entity, as is evidenced by American religious conversions taking place in prisons. When ex-offenders return to the community, their rate of reconviction is as high as those who have not experienced being born again while confined. There is no conflict on this point of morality, then, between the atheist and the theist. We cannot demonstrate divine intervention. We can only demonstrate that what is divine within us must be nurtured to its full capacity. And in this awareness, we come to condemn all forms of brutality committed against our fellow humans and creatures.

The only difference regarding our moral code is its assumed source. Is it within our DNA, or is it a supernatural gift from God? Conflict between the atheist and the theist comes from assuming that the Moral Law works from an external source, rather than observing how it emerges from our own psyches. As we document the emergence of morality through natural processes, we come to know either God's work, or the work of nature. It is the same.

I never understood why some believers insist that God can only work as an external source rather than through the natural evolutionary design that guides all creatures, a design the theist attributes to God, and a design the atheist attributes to chance.

Glen A. Just

Once we get rid of the idea that God has limited abilities or can only work in magical ways, this conflict between the theist and atheist is eliminated, at least for many of us. As that wonderful crafter of prose, Coelhoe, said in the Alchemist:

> "I have known true alchemists," the alchemist continued. "... they understood that when something evolves, everything around that thing evolves as well."

EPILOGUE

THOUGHTS ON EXPERIENTIAL PSYCHOLOGY

I envision this delightful degree program where sincere students from different religions, philosophies, and worldviews come together to explore their existential realities; students who are not afraid of who they are, and are willing to discover what wonderful new worlds lie waiting to be revealed within their psyches. Together they would study and review basics similar to my self-directed life of discovery of hypnosis, self-hypnosis, group hypnosis, behavior modification and cognitive restructuring, basic neural-psychology, developmental psychology, and neural philosophy, comparative world religions, social thought both East and West, and an objective, historical understanding of our own beliefs and religious orientations. This would include the study of atheism in terms of what I have called the faith of non-faith, for denying the possibility of a Cosmic Sentient Being, or Beings, with today's level of technology seems a bit premature. Perhaps discovering this Being within ourselves is something akin to the motivations of the pre-scientific minds of the Gnostics.

Field work, or internships, would be guided out-of-body experiences, dream programming, other directed and then self-induced states of intense concentration for study purposes, control over natural body functions such as pain and heart rate,

Glen A. Just

speaking-in-tongues, channeling, or generally stated, the types of self-taught experiences I have discussed in this book and *Autobiography of a Ghost.* I would love to see unobtrusive technology watch the inner workings of our brains as we become the bear, channel, engage in automatic writing, or fly to the moon and beyond. I know from personal experience that experiential research can be brought under the microscope, or more appropriately, using unobtrusive technologies such as fMRIs, and feel strongly that in doing so, we will finally bring religion our of its Dark Ages.

We now have the ability to more fully explain and evaluate the normal brain functions of ASC, and need not sit around in our isolated offices in academe and throw spears at one another from superior respective chairs of the theist or atheist, or even worse, throw spears at each other from the assumed superior and lofty heights of our preferred faiths. It is time that we separate our natural brain functions from whatever else there may be. I have offered a yardstick by which we can measure altered realities, as well as identifying the very natural human behavior of the mystics, through *Autobiography of a Ghost,* and now, in this sequel. Forgive me if I have not always made this measurement yardstick clear along the way.

Our natural ability to separate areas of mental functioning from one another, and reconfigure them in creative ways, permits us to experience out-of-body projections, speaking-in-tongues, dream programming, (reincarnation) and other related but natural states of altered reality. These experiences can be exhilarating or terrifying depending on whether or not we control them or think we are being controlled by good or evil forces in the spirit world, forces that exist independent of our bodies and are forces "out there."

It is often comforting for the mentally ill who cannot control the voices or mental images that come to them, to learn that similar experiences are just inside their heads. How much more helpful it would be to use the experiential techniques described in "Ghost" to give them control over these daytime nightmares.

As mental health workers, we discover the internal world of the mentally ill, or chemically addicted, unfolding as we engage them in treatment - an internal world they share with us when it

194

is safe. I think many mentally ill people can be given new self-control through the equivalent of carefully taught dream programming, and an enhanced ability to consciously switch unwanted brain routines to a more direct form of behavior modification for the brain, if you will, and in the process, increase brain flexibility by teaching individuals how to assume self-control of various altered realities, integrating fragmented neural functions, and stabilizing brain chemistry. I know from personal experiments that brain and mind modifications can be reshaped simply, cheaply, and quickly brought under self control. Achieving good mental health through self-directed and self-controlled interventions was the key to my recovery, and these effects have lasted a life time.

Lastly, psychopathic conditions exist when the self identifies with the Self and not others. We have yet to explore the experimental reconditioning of psychopaths using the techniques I've presented. It would be interesting to attempt connecting the psychopaths disconnected treads of individuality to the rest of humanity through similar brain reconditioning methods. Natural reinforcement of punishable behavior can be established through internally directed feedback loops.

I know from self-directed experiments in my early college days that we can learn to control and adjust brain chemistry in areas such as anxiety and depression this way, and that these adjustments are long lasting. To what degree damaged brains can be repaired when areas such as the amygdale are not fully expressed awaits new research. However, I am a good case study of one in terms of what can happen over one's lifetime when we learn to stabilize brain chemistry by ridding ourselves of trauma, anxiety, and depression, as well as ghosts and spirits.

Symptoms that I exhibited when hospitalized as a two year old support at least limited brain damage from smothering. I lost my early ability to speak and walk and had to relearn each upon return to community. My behavioral history further supports these smothering attacks as occurring over an extended period of time, as I learned to cup my hand over my nose and mouth in order to continue breathing at a reduced rate. I experienced "epileptic fits" as described by my Mother with some effects such as fainting recalled as late as age eight. Other

195

aspects of early behavioral conditioning continued lifelong, such as anxiety in small, closed spaces, and immediate emotional reactions to strong authoritarian personalities.

TESTABLE HYPOTHESES

Routines of cognitive-behavioral modification coupled with newly restructured neural pathways, as evidenced by my own experiences, await further study and confirmation. In this light, I offer some testable hypotheses:

Hypothesis 1: **Altered reality experiences bring neural pathways in our brains together in unusual combinations.** For example, I am suggesting that the neural mechanism behind the shamanic experience such as leaving one's body is due to unusual or abnormal neural networks being configured, and that these pathways can be documented by unobtrusive measures such as fMRIs.

Discussion: A. Damasio and other neural scientists have grounded consciousness and self in the body and brain. From an experiential view, this has always been my perception, and is the only explanation that supports my own altered reality states. I will repeat three examples to support this contention: Zen driving, flying to the moon, and flying out-of-body to the beginning of time – what I've called the Cosmic Shaman episode.

At eight years of age, I decided to sit on the moon after witnessing an attempt by my father to chop off my brother's head. I was too young to understand that my body was not still attached as I flew toward the moon, began to experience the extreme cold, shivered, and developed fear of becoming lost if I journeyed all the way. I recount this subjective understanding to show the reader how real this experience was for a naïve child. My in-route journey included visual contact with both the moon and the earth. What I did not process is the fact that my understanding of geography would not possibly have permitted me to navigate back home from interstellar space.

In the act of Zen driving, I separate my body from mind and let it join with the car as though the two were fused. This created a sensation of flying a couple feet above the highway, and was even more pleasant than flying at a great height above the earth, which I obviously could not do driving my car in a normal state of consciousness. Of course, all of this was a generated subjective reality in my mind, and I was fully aware of creating and controlling the process. Nevertheless, my mind had to open different neural pathways than those used for ordinary driving and shut down others. My attention remained focused on the road and traffic as I glided along with a mind that felt totally detached from my body. I was consciously aware that my body was detached as I effortlessly floated above the highway and enjoyed the sense of flying. My mind used my body as reference as it relaxed and let my body guide the car by itself. The two moved together, but without any sense of being directly connected. In the same sense that the reader knows that he or she is reading these words while at the same time their mind is comfortably attached to their body (head).

My subjective reality was a detached body fused with the car automatically controlling the event, while my mind took a holiday and enjoyed watching the beautiful moonlit scenery along Wisconsin's rolling hills and wooded landscapes. I suppose a curious state for someone who doesn't practice this kind of driving, but a feeling state that joggers and motorcycle riders often report and know from firsthand experience.

Last, I separated myself from body, and flew back to the beginning of time; thirteen billion, seven hundred million years, or thereabout, and experienced the beginning of time by having the sensation of physically hitting the plasma wall of our universe's beginning. I report this journey in more detail in *Autobiography of a Ghost,* so I will not elaborate again.

I was subjectively and experientially exploring quantum entanglement, the Big Bang, and faster than light movement in this exercise. I observed all stages of the universe unfolding over its history, and then returned instantly to my easy chair – where I was still comfortably reclining in my living room on a cold winter's day. I no longer had to worry about getting lost. My eight year old child's understanding of altered realities had been improved considerably. I knew that my body was my reference point as psychology and the neural sciences had added this understanding over the years.

The self in either normal or altered reality states uses its own body for reference. Those of us who journey out-of-body never get lost. How could it be? Whether we think of our journeys as astral travel, travelling to a previous life (reincarnation), or playing with spirit possession, the return to body is automatic. It cannot be otherwise.

Hypothesis 2: Dream Programming uses all normal brain functions as do common dreams with the exception being that when the dream sequence starts, there will be detectable input from neural centers responsible for consciousness. Meaning, immediately after the brain initiates a normal dream sequence, there will be input from conscious neural centers directing dream programming. (I assume that input is non-local by the conscious brain, even though I think of this aspect of my conscious self occurring through my Controller.) However, this conscious input may diminish once a routine is established.

Dream Programming, where we consciously use hypnosis or self-hypnosis to plant movie sequences in normal nighttime dreams, or switch the story in a specific dream, does not activate programmed dreams, but merely creates content for them. I used self-hypnosis to switch dream content when nightmares emerged, but I did not consciously create the initial dream from scratch, or preset sleep time periods for their expression.   ,

I assume that conscious input from our performing brains will be limited in dream programming, as I do not experientially detect any extra effort or energy expenditure in this process. Whatever my brain is about in the normal act of dreaming, it continues to fulfill this function. However, the impact of nightmares as "object" input that initiates sweating and changes in brain chemistry from recalled trauma does not occur when dream programs take over dream content. (I use "object" in the same sense as Damasio meaning any internal or external event recorded by our brains.)

Hypothesis 3: Neural pathways and brain chemical levels are permanently modified through the use of dream programming; and, neural responses supporting the brain's recycling of traumatic episodes will be permanently modified and weakened.

I assume that physical body and brain are being modified, in the sense of "behavior modification" as used by psychologists, by exercising direct control over nightmares, or other traumas that normally creates tension within our muscles, vascular dilation or the brains production of chemicals that create a multitude of undesirable physical effects, especially those effects that have long-term deleterious impact on body and brain. I further assume that this therapeutic process is superior to the use of artificial drugs to control depression and anxiety as permanent modifications are occurring in the brain that permit improved baseline responses and behavior by the organism.

To express this idea another way, when I think of how I developed neural and body conditioning, I used my mind to teach my brain and body to alter physiological responses associated with anxiety, depression, paranoid perceptions, and hyper-vigilance. However, I first taught my mind how to take control of automatic and autonomic functions such as pain responses, breathing, and blood vessel constriction and dilation.

This was an incremental learning sequence for my mind. I knew from experience that self-hypnosis was not something I could immediately create with full effect, and in similar fashion, I approached retraining my brain in incremental steps. The best learning sequences for extended concentration, control over autonomic functions, and attention span need to be determined experimentally.

Hypothesis 4: Employing shamanic techniques of self-control, which are also used in certain types of meditation, can either prevent or reduce the effects of childhood schizophrenia.

Glen A. Just

My Minnesota Multiphasic Personality Inventory (MMPI) registered in the critical statistical range for this disorder when I was twenty-one years of age. After practicing a self-programmed regimen that included dream programming, extended periods of concentration for up to eight hours, as well as assuming control over normal autonomic functions such as pain, my MMPI profile returned to normal at the end of three years. I suspect that this profile was within normal ranges within one year, but I did not test myself as I was unaware of this profile until I was almost ready to graduate at the end of my senior year. It appears reasonable to assume that similar reprogramming of neural circuits may return brain chemical levels to normal and stop the progression of this disorder.

Sophia Vinogradov at the University of California, San Francisco, notes that there is marked improvement of schizophrenics with intensive and progressive cognitive training. Michael Merzenich reports that the constant surge of neurotransmitters dopamine and norepinephrine gradually poisons the brain. These examples support the fact that excessive chemical outputs by the brain create progressive deterioration of neural functions that exacerbate the symptoms of schizophrenia.

Physically fraying neurons and killing of dendrites is part of this process. The techniques I self-administered may apply to other related disorders as well, and I think offers promising direction for future exploration as they involve cognitive restructuring and stabilization of brain chemistry. Additionally, they are routines that can be self-administered, low cost, and don't require any equipment. Obviously, the medical community would want to establish these routines, and confirm under what conditions they are effective.

Hypothesis 5: Born again religious adherents, speakers-in-tongues, individuals possessed by spirits, and those with uncontrollable psychotic episodes will show similar brain chemical responses as those practicing ASC under controlled conditions.

Speaking-in-tongues activates endorphins and other brain chemicals that produce a super runners high, and can become as

200

addicting as intermittent variable reinforcement provided by modern casino slot machines. Individuals who seek these experiences look forward to revival meetings the way slot machine addicts look forward to their next play time fix. Their brains and bodies become excited just thinking about the next episode. I was intrigued as a youngster just entering grade school with this phenomenon, and still have memories of the ecstatic state I was being exposed to, as church members spoke-in-tongues, and often rolled around on the floor in unrequited bliss.

Spirit possession, where the individual feels controlled by something coming from "out there," seems to activate the same neural responses and subjective reactions as that of individuals who are experiencing psychotic episodes where self-control is lost. This sense of possession has been common enough historically for Christian priests and world shamans to develop effective intervention strategies. It is also an experience that happens when individuals lose control from street drugs.

An acquaintance of mine recounted an experience where he was losing his fight against a spirit that was attempting to enter his body, and began to flail about in panic. One of his fellow practitioners grabbed him, and this act of touching immediately returned his self control. In other words, he was grounded to his body by his friends touch; physical contact reactivated self-control that comes with normal neural processing. At least, that is the interpretation that seems most plausible to me. (The loss of control was street drug induced.)

Uncontrollable episodes of mental illness were part of my childhood, and I previously recounted an encounter with "mind controlling cracks" in my hometown's sidewalk. The control over my mind by the sidewalk cracks became increasingly stronger, until one day, in utter frustration, and with the realization that no one would listen to or help me, I began to stamp them furiously. In retrospect, this physical contact, grounding, permitted a rather rapid return to self-control. Once I realized my superior control to that of the sidewalk cracks, they didn't have a chance.

Neural science and developmental psychology have brought considerable insight as to how my self-therapies worked. It

Glen A. Just

seems reasonable to assume that these techniques will also work for others. The mystic mind does have many bright sides. I have come to believe that consciously using and controlling ASC experiences opens up fuller use of coordinated brain functions, and is itself related to enhanced creativity. At least, individuals who enter ASC states are revealing relationships that appear uncommon and tempting to their followers.

Hypothesis 6: Teaching individuals self-control over their bodies and minds is an effective technique for the reduction of anxiety and depression.

Clinical levels of anxiety where I sat immobilized in university classroom test situations, and depression, where I set out to commit suicide, were eliminated when I taught myself how to use extended periods of concentration for study, and to gain control over pain to a degree where I could stick pins in myself without feeling. I know from personal experience with self-taught meditation that feelings of contentment, centeredness, and positive moods can be maintained and enhanced though meditative states induced through self-hypnosis. I expect the results are similar to those of Transcendental Meditation.

Thus, it seems a little backwards to simply employ pharmaceuticals for this purpose, thereby creating drug dependencies without simultaneously teaching the client to employ techniques of self-control. I skipped unavailable and unaffordable medications by using the methods discussed above, and the effects have lasted over fifty years.

Hypothesis 7: Self-hypnotic routines as presented can improve one's sense of being whole, and experiencing unity throughout one's life and social space, thereby significantly enhancing quality of life. Clearing one's mind of clutter permits easier and quicker access to projected feelings such as empathy, thereby increasing the social bonds to an ever larger living world.

I think of some of my self-hypnotic routines as a type of neural flooding, in which I am breaking down neural compartments where triggers for anxiety and depression are

202

centered, and opening the brain's neural pathways so one experiences a connection with the All. I use the expression All to mean the state I subjectively feel when I open my mind to let any thought or feeling flood in and overcome my focused consciousness. In other words, I am letting my mind simultaneously experience all the inputs from its body, or, if not all inputs, experiencing enough to overwhelm normal processing, hence my use of the word flooding. It is an experience interpreted by those having ASC episodes that brings them into contact with the supernatural. (Flooding can also be experienced as "nothingness.")

Previously when I experienced a clinical level of anxiety, my focus would be on the anxiety, thereby giving my anxiety greater prominence in my "Now" centered consciousness, and creating a similar dysfunctional counterpart to the casino slot machine addict or alcoholic's focus on their object of choice. Once I taught myself extended periods of concentration, I could switch my focus away from anxiety or depression to any other object of choice, and thus pursue a different method to achieve positive thinking. I learned that anxiety was just one neural pattern in my brain, and it was a pathway I could choose to express, or choose not to express.

Neural flooding subjectively feels like one is connecting every neuron in the brain at the same time. I actually close my eyes and have a sense of being in an immense star field at the beginning when I permit flooding to emerge. The billions of neurons are like little points of light that I can visually scan; a very pleasant sensation with relaxation increasing with length of exposure. It is a little like watching a beautiful, clear, and star lit sky on a warm summer's night. I can achieve the same effect by focusing on the imagined space between an atomic nucleus and assumed electron shell. For me, this is the ultimate emptiness where nothing exists physically, although I know there is a force field operating. Flooding or the void; totality or nothing; each is equal to the other, and generates the same effect.

What I experience in terms of my brain's neuronal functions is a near total sense of unity and oneness. If I concentrate long and hard, nothing else exists. It is the type of oneness or union with God reported by various religious practitioners. From personal experience, I know that my brain chemistry is brought into relaxed-state ranges by these techniques as I become calm, have a pleasant sense of well being, and under some circumstances, especially if I have had a traumatic event happen or been under extreme stress, a sense of euphoria will emerge. Some people report this experience when praying, and have a sense of being united with their Supreme Being.

Hypothesis 8: Tested psychopaths can increase their social and emotional identification with others by being purposefully taught how to project their sense of self onto others, thereby coming to subjectively identify with other's feelings. But first, a qualifier: I believe that the entire limbic system must be fully developed, or within a few percentage points of being fully developed, for these routines to work. A type of therapy I hope neural scientists like Antonio Damasio will pursue.

My work with populations in correctional treatment programs, which I have either developed or observed, support the fact that a significant number of tested psychopaths develop consciences that fall in the normal range by their late thirties or so. My personal experience tells me that those recovering from this diagnosis, individuals who come to exhibit normal moral and ethical behavior, have a condition socially induced from defective environments. Therefore, I am proposing that new neuronal connections can be established that will support the self's ability to be projected onto others by directly modifying behavioral routines in a manner similar to those that I have reported; intra-psychic modifications of patterned neuronal expression. I am assuming the defect lies in scrambled neural pathways for the so-called pseudo-psychopath. The distinction, then, is between psychopaths with permanent organic damage to their brains, versus others who have inadequate neural development due to learned routines, the social psychopath.

Hypothesis 9: Alcoholics and drug addicts who have intense or born-again religious episodes, are expressing the same neuronal pathway modifications as those of us naturally experiencing altered realities.

In *Autobiography of a Ghost,* I compare group drug trips and their seeming reality to religious mystic experiences where individuals feel they are visiting a former life or collectively viewing the same phenomenon, the appearance of Mother Mary for example. The former example I gave was that of a group of my university students in the 1970s getting "high" on hallucinogens on a hot summer day and sitting on an imagined, but subjectively real, iceberg in order to cool off. I also gave an example of a peyote ceremony in the Native American Church where a group of a hundred or so attendees simultaneously experienced the return of a deceased member. If individuals have the same cultural expectations, the experience can be shared with any number of people. I suggested, therefore, that numbers cannot be used to verify the reality of altered states, nor can they be used as proof that God has intervened. We have many such collective histories reported in religious literature.

Experiences of altered realities like this can be very creative, where creatures or deities come to speak directly to the Initiate; Saint Paul being a good example. Damasio states in *The Feeling of What Happens* that our brains can use internally created "objects" as factually as externally experienced objects (Chapter 7.) It is little wonder that alcoholics and drug addicts are drawn to twelve step programs; their religious nature has been activated, and the presence of God confirmed. If we are by nature programmed by our DNA to have a religious nature, then a multitude of triggers can activate this awareness, including drugs and alcohol. For the drug dependent atheist, his or her Higher Power becomes the Unified Self.

Hypothesis 10: The Moral Law emerges from the mind naturally when adequate social support and nurturing is provided. I think support already abundantly exists for this assumption, but there are a number of ways it can be confirmed.

Criminal populations who are converted to religion do not improve their out of prison behavior if they return to dysfunctional environments. Social support for a new lifestyle must be provided, as prayer alone is ineffective. I believe that numerous sources support morality as emerging from our own psyches, with this moral emergent coming into being only when

Glen A. Just

adequate nurturing and social, environmental support is provided. If moral behavior were to come from outside, prayer and conversion would suffice. If God or nature has placed this program (algorithm) in our genes, we are obliged to access it. Studies in the Oregon prison system at the turn of the 21st Century support the position that prayer must be coupled with conscious involvement and support if conversion is to produce positive behavioral changes.

Developmental psychology is demonstrating stages of adult maturity, and these stages exhibit progressive moral development with aging. I have used my own history of physical violence in my youth as an example. I naturally came to reject my hair-trigger fighting responses as anxiety, depression, and hyper-vigilance were brought under control, as I integrated self, and stabilized my personality profile.

Lastly, I believe that other highly developed species such as dolphins demonstrate the Moral Law when they push a drowning human swimmer to the surface. Apparently their ability to scan swimmers and identify oxygen deprivation activates this innate (group or socially based) moral response that is built into their brains. Hence, my contention that the Moral Law is an emergent built into the algorithm of our DNA, an algorithm that is not exclusive to humans, or most likely, just as common to extra-terrestrials, creating an answer to the question of, "Where are they?"

SUMMARY

The above hypotheses can be made operational fairly easily. I am advocating two approaches to ongoing research that I believe will help reconcile differences between some members of both the scientific and religious communities: 1) A university or institute-centered program based on experiential research where students learn to create and control altered reality the way I have; plus, 2) directly testing and integrating across disciplines, hypotheses like those presented above.

I have contended throughout this book that we humans have an innate religious nature that cannot be denied, that denial of our religious nature continues to further conflict on all fronts between individuals and cultures, and that recognition and confirmation of this DNA emergent is necessary if we are to achieve interpersonal and world peace.

I have taken traditional religions to task for denying that our basic religious nature is built into our evolutionary self. Personally, I feel that denying the beauty of our evolving universe, the beauty of evolving life, the beauty of evolving humanity, is an act that potentially separates us from a knowable God or Cosmic Presence. Why do so many of our fellow humans insist that the magician's rod drawing circles in the dirt is the only manner that a Cosmic Intelligence can use to express Itself? Who insist that science is in conflict with religion, and in so doing, imply that the laws of nature are man-made.

I do not profess to know answers to these ultimate questions of reality, but I am sure that they cannot be answered with historical statements that support dogmas espoused by world religions. If one accepts that our basic natures are given to us by God, why should we fear an honest search? If one believes that nature alone has created human beings, why should we fear an honest quest exploring this religious nature? I believe the theist and atheist must stop beating each other over the head, and become open to a final process of scientific exploration.

Finally, I experience a natural development of religious thought throughout recorded history. Ancient Israel had many gods and Yahwehs. The concept of monolatry gradually emerged in the ancient world, where one god was given prominence over the others. Eventually this one god became backed by state and military power, and was imposed on large numbers of individuals. And finally, in the contemporary era, a "true" concept of monotheism begins to emerge. That concept, Entity, is an Intelligent Universe: a timeless, formless, ever present Spirit that exists throughout the cosmos. And we therefore come to live in a Cosmocentric Universive as Homo religiosus.

207

Glen A. Just

Schneider, in *Beyond Monotheism,* notes that the word monotheism itself did not appear until More used it in 1690 "...as an epithet internal to Christianity, directed against early Unitarian ideas of God-identity." (19) Further, in the early 19th Century, it was used only for the third time. "Indeed, monotheism as such has never really existed anywhere except in ideology, and so can only function polemically." (25) Schneider very poignantly brings our focus to the present struggle for legitimacy going on with Trinitarians. It seems that the historical march toward the One-God has reached a critical point of no return.

In conclusion, as civilization marches on, the world of science creates an ever larger, integrated knowledge base, and from this whirlpool of consilience emerges the Oneness found within the self that cannot be denied. How could it be that human nature is not part of nature, and the remaining final question is a controversial one between God and chance? Here, I contend, lies a degree of reconciliation between science and religion that we should refine, embrace, and then move on to the next level of human spiritual development and comfort.

Let me close with some thoughts from Davies and Evans: (Davies, 207), "It seems to me that a unique mathematical theory that makes no reference to life, but that nevertheless yields life, is as unbelievable as seeing a face leap out from among the early digits of @." (He speaks of an experiment where @ is running and a face appears in the first two minutes.)

p. 226: "But there is no reason in principle why life and mind cannot, over eons, transform the structure of the universe on a very large scale."

p. 228: "It seems clear that life (and, as I shall argue in what follows, mind and culture too) is an equally significant step on the path of cosmic evolution."

p. 233: "To sum it up in a phrase, life as we observe it today is 1 percent physics and 99 percent history."

p. 236: "But what happens if we relinquish this idealized Platonic view of the laws of physics." (Davies supports a fairly strong Anthropic Cosmological Principle.)

(Bergen Evans), 274: "The mist of mysticism has always provided good cover for those who do not want their actions too closely looked into."

BIBLIOGRAPHY

Andrews, D., Bonta, J. (1998). The Psychology of Criminal Conduct. Cincinnati: Anderson Publishing Company.

Aristotle. (1996). The Nicomachean Ethics. Hertfordshire: Wordsworth Classics of World Literature.

Barber, B. (1952). Science and the social order. Glencoe: The Free Press.

Barkalaja, A. Shamanism as Information Design (21-55)) in Leete, A., Firnhaber, R.P., eds. (2004). Boca Raton: Brown Walker Press.

Bloom, F.E., Beal, M.F., Kupfer, D.J. (2003). The Dana Guide To Brain Health. New York: Free Press.

Butz, J. J. (2005). The Brother of Jesus and the Lost Teachings of Christianity. Rochester, Vermont: Inner Traditions.

Casti, J. (1994). Complexification. New York: Harper Collins.

Cohen, J.B. (1985). Revolution in Science. Cambridge, Massachusetts: Harvard University Press.

Collins, F.S. (2007). The Language of God. New York: Free Press Paperback.

Comte, A. (1855). The positive philosophy of Auguste Comte. Trans. Harriet Martineau. New York: Calvin Blanchard.

Damasio, A. R. (1994). Descartes Error: Emotion, Reason, and the Human Brain. New York: Grossman/Putnam

Damasio, A. R. (1999). The Feeling of What Happens. Orlando: Houghton Mifflin Harcourt Publishing.

Damasio, A. R. (2003). Looking for Spinoza: Joy, Sorrow, and the Feeling Brain. Orlando: Harcourt Publishers.

Davies, P. (2007). Cosmic Jackpot: Why Our Universe Is Just Right for Life. New York: Houghton Mifflin Company.

Dawkins, R. (1989). The Selfish Gene. Oxford: Oxford University Press.

Dawkins, R. (2006). The God Delusion. New York: Houghton Mifflin.

Doide, N. (2007). The Brain that changes Itself: Stories of Personal Triumph from the Frontiers of Brain Science. New York: Viking.

210

Ehrman, B. D. (2003). Lost Christianities: The Battle of Scripture and the Faiths We Never Knew. New Oxford: Oxford University Press.

Evans, B. (1947). The Natural History of Nonsense. New York: Alfred A. Knopf.

Firnhaber, R. P. Mapping the ASC: A Cultural-Physiological Construct (84-119) in Leete, A., Firnhaber, R.P., eds. (2004). Boca Raton: Brown Walker Press.

Frank, P. (1947). Einstein, his life and times. New York: Alfred A. Knopf.

Freud, S. (1997). The Interpretation of Dreams. Hertfordshire: Wordsworth Classics of World Literature.

Gardner, J. (2007). The Intelligent Universe. Franklin Lakes: New Page Books.

Gibran, K. (1979). The Prophet. New York: Alfred A. Knopf.

Green, B. (2000). The Elegant Universe. New York: Vintage.

Green, B. (2004). The Fabric Of The Cosmos: Space, Time, And The Texture Of Reality.
New York: Vintage Books.

Griffin, D. R. (1989). Archetypal Process: Self and Devine in Whitehead, Jung, and Hillman. Evanston: Northwestern University Press.

Guth, A. (1997). The Inflationary Universe. Reading: Perseus.

Hare, R. (1993). Without Conscience: The Disturbing World of the Psychopaths Among Us. New York: Guilford Press.

Harris, S. (2005), The End of Faith: Religion, Terror, and the Future of Reason. New York: W. W. Norton & Company.

Hawking, S. (1988). A Brief History of Time. London: Bantam.

Hemingway, E. (2004). For Whom the Bell Tolls. London: Arrow Books.

Hoeller, S. A. (2003), Gnosticism: New Light On The Ancient Tradition Of Inner
Knowing. Wheaton: The Theosophical Publishing House.

Hooper, D. (2006). Dark Cosmos: In Search of Our Universe's Missing Mass and Energy. New York: Smithsonian Books, HarperCollins.

Humphrey, N. (2002). The Mind Made Flesh: Frontiers of Psychology and Evolution. Oxford: Oxford University Press.

Glen A. Just

Just, G. A. (2009). Autobiography of a Ghost. Mankato, MN: Eagle Entertainment USA.

Kaku, M. (1994). Hyperspace. New York: Oxford University Press.

Kaku, M. (2005). Parallel Worlds: A Journey Through Creation, Higher Dimensions, and the Future of the Cosmos. New York: Anchor Books.

Kauffman, S. (1993). The Origin of Order. Oxford: Oxford University Press.

Kirsch, J. (2005). God Against The Gods. Penguin Books: New York.

Kuhn, T.S. (1962). The structure of scientific revolutions. Chicago: The University of Chicago Press.

Lakoff, B., Johnson, M. (1999). Philosophy In The Flesh: The Embodied Mind And Its Challenge To Western Thought. New York: Basic Books.

LeDoux, J. (1996). The Emotional Brain: The Mysterious Underpinnings of Emotional Life. New York: Simon & Schuster Paperbacks.

LeDoux, J. (2003). Synaptic Self: How Our Brains Become Who We Are. New York: Penguin.

Leete, A., Firnhaber, R.P., eds. (2004). Shamanism in the Interdisciplinary Context. Boca Raton: Brown Walker Press.

Mead, G. H. (1936). Movements of thought in the nineteenth century. Chicago: University of Chicago Press.

Mero, L. (1998). Moral Calculations: Game Theory, Logic, and Human Frailty. New York: Copernicus.

Moffett, S. (2006). The Three-Pound Enigma: The Human Brain and the Quest to Unlock Its Mysteries. Chapel Hill, NC: Algonquin Books.

Narby, J. Shamanism in Science (14-20) in Leete, A., Firnhaber, R.P., eds. (2004). Boca Raton: Brown Walker Press.

Penrose, R. (1994). Shadows of the Mind: A Search for the Missing Science of Consciousness. Oxford: Oxford University Press.

Piaget, J. (1962). Play, Dream, and Imitation in Childhood. New York: Norton.,

Picknett, L. (2004). Mary Magdalene. New York: Carroll & Graf Publishers.

Pierce, J.H. (2006). The Owners Manual for the Brain: Everyday Applications from Mind-Body Research. Austin: Bard Press.

Prigogine, I. (1980). From being to becoming: time and complexity in the physical sciences. San Francisco: W. H. Freeman and Company.

Radin, P. (1957). Primitive Man as Philosopher. New York: Dover Publications.

Restak, R. (2006). The Naked Brain: How the Emerging Neurosociety Is Changing How We Live, Work, and Love. New York: Harmony Books.

Robinson, J.M. (1990). The Nag Hammadi Library. New York: HarperCollins Publishers.

Satinover, J. (2001). The Quantum Brain: The Search for Freedom and the Next Generation of Man. New York: John Wiley & Sons, Inc.

Schneider, L. C. (2008). Beyond Monotheism: A Theology of Multiplicity. New York: Routledge.

Smolin, L. (1997). The Life of the Cosmos. Oxford: Oxford University Press.

Spinoza. (1955). The Ethics. New York: Dover Press.

Stanford, C. (2001). Significant Others: The Ape-Human Continuum and the Quest for Human Nature. New York: Basic Books.

Star, C. G. (1991). A History of the Ancient World. New York: Oxford University Press.

Steltenkamp, M. (1993). Black Elk: Holy Man of the Oglala. Norman: University of Oklahoma Press.

Tipler, F. (1994). The Physics of Immortality. New York: Doubleday.

Weatherford, J. (2004). Genghis Khan and the Making of the Modern World. New York: Three Rivers Press.

Wilhelmi, B. Differentiations: A Shamanic Reading of the Gospels (142-148) in Leete, A., Firnhaber, R.P., eds. (2004). Boca Raton: Brown Walker Press.

Wilson, E. O. (1999). Consilience: The Unity of Knowledge. New York: Vintage

www.ingramcontent.com/pod-product-compliance
Lightning Source LLC
Chambersburg PA
CBHW030924090426
42737CB00007B/315